As both a Western Medical Doctor and a long time Chi Kung practitioner I believe that Sifu Spinicchia's, *Wonders of Chi Kung*, is a fascinating and profound contribution to helping people understand how relevant Chi Kung can be in their lives. Unlike many volumes on the subject this book is written in an easy to read manner making it accessible to people from all walks of life including those who may have not been interested in Chi Kung or any type of Eastern Art. This book can be quickly read in a couple of hours making it an easy introduction. The author demystifies an Ancient Art while focusing on its practical applications for people in the fast paced Western world. I highly recommend this book and in fact encourage my own interested patients to get a copy. At a minimum, readers can enlighten themselves on what Chi Kung is as the International Media begins to reference the Art more and more. At best, readers will be inspired by this book to make significant improvements in their lives.

Damian Kissey, M.D.

The Wonders of Chi Kung

Relieving Stress and Unlocking Glowing Health and Vitality

Second Edition

By Anthony Spinicchia

ISBN 978-0-578-02487-5

$14.95
ISBN 978-0-578-02487-5
51495>

9 780578 024875

Sifu Anthony Spinicchia

**Anthony Spinicchia with his teacher the World Famous
Shaolin Grandmaster Wong Kiew Kit**

Anthony Spinicchia is 44 years of age and teaches Shaolin Chi Kung to individuals, groups and organizations and conducts public and private lectures on this incredible art and how it is relevant to people today. He also provides personalized Chi Therapy to people suffering from chronic, painful and life threatening conditions. His website is www.wondersofchikung.com .

Mr. Spinicchia's popular lectures and presentations are known for being informative, interesting and fun. If you would like a presentation to your group or organization on Chi Kung and how it is relevant to them or you are interested in Chi Therapy for yourself or a loved one you may contact Mr. Spinicchia via the contact info contained in his websites or at

Anthony Spinicchia
7380 S. Eastern Avenue
#124-282
Las Vegas, NV 89123
United States

Legal Disclaimer regarding instructions contained in this book. Chi Kung is practiced gently and carefully and is not complicated. It is harmless unless someone recklessly disregards instruction or obvious warning signs of improper practice. Results can only be obtained by regular, consistent and correct practice. These factors are controlled by the practitioner. If you have any concerns about practicing Chi Kung due to your health status or any illness that you may have you should consult your licensed Medical Physician before practicing Chi Kung. The most effective and safest way to learn and practice Chi Kung is directly from a competent instructor. The author and publisher take no responsibility in how a reader interprets the instructions in this book and how or whether the reader practices unsuccessfully or for any undesirable results obtained.

Table of Contents

Acknowledgments

Everything I have learned about Chi Kung came from only two sources-my teacher and my own practice. The first source, my teacher, Sifu Wong Kiew Kit of Kedah, Malaysia, literally taught me everything I would ever need to know about Chi Kung, specifically Shaolin Chi Kung. Sifu comes from a long line of Shaolin Masters who have dedicatedly preserved a rare and exclusive art for hundreds of years.

Beyond teaching me how to practice correctly in order to get profound results in a safe manner, Sifu "transmitted" the art to me "heart to heart". This is in the Eastern tradition of Shaolin and other rare and profound arts. For the past 9 years I have traveled to his home frequently to learn directly and personally from Sifu in hundreds of hours of training. Learning this incredible art has enhanced and changed my life so profoundly for the better that I will always be grateful to Sifu and the long line of Shaolin Masters before him. I can never repay them for this gift. However, sharing our art with you and many others is one attempt to do so.

My second source of learning is my own practice. This is also in the Shaolin tradition. One can read about Chi Kung from authoritative sources and watch videos and attend seminars and classes but understanding only comes from dedicated practice. Those who have practiced a profound art in a dedicated manner know this. With practice one is able to achieve the fantastic results that Chi Kung promises and understand the reasoning for the principles and guidelines that one's teacher has provided.

I also wish to thank one of Sifu's long time students, Ryan Berg. Ryan encouraged me to write the first edition of this book so that it can inspire others to get the benefits that we have received over our many years of practice. Thanks Ryan for helping me fulfill my vision of helping as many people as possible to overcome illness and enjoy a life of joy and fulfillment.

Anthony Spinicchia
May 2009

Dedicated to my Mom

Introduction:

How Reducing Stress Will Change Your Life

As you may have be aware stress is more than just a subtle pressure pushing you forward to accomplish the things that you want. Left unchecked, stress can become a dangerous and destructive force in all aspects of your life, from the quality of work you do, the interactions you have each day with the people you care about, the overall sense of well being you feel, to virtually every aspect of your physical health.

The link between stress and how our body and mind function is becoming less and less of a mystery each day. We now know from Western Medical research that stress even affects the expression of our genes, the core building blocks of all the processes in our body. We know it affects many of the key chemicals that control how we feel, think, and how our body fights disease.

Furthermore, the mystery of how to alleviate this harmful stress is becoming clearer through observations made in modern science. Many modern, scientific studies have been conducted on ancient health practices, and in particular a powerful ancient health practice known as Chi Kung, showing many amazing stress relieving results. (Chi Kung is pronounced chee-kung and is also spelled as Qigong)

But the stress relieving, health enhancing powers of Chi Kung are not new. And while it is wonderful that modern medicine and science are now confirming its power, practitioners of Chi Kung have experienced its wondrous benefits firsthand for thousands of years.

Over this time, Chi Kung has been refined into what many believe is the most powerful and effective system for maintaining vibrant health and vitality in both mind and body well into old age despite demanding, seemingly stressful lifestyles.

Today Chi Kung is practiced by thousands of people who live out what many would consider extremely stressful lives. Yet, through practicing Chi Kung, these people are able to navigate the pressures in their life with an unmatched ease and grace allowing them to fully enjoy their work, play, and all the challenges that come with them.

More than just being able to feel relaxed, Chi Kung helps CEO's, physicians, government officials, teachers, famous entertainers, world class athletes and other people from all walks of life perform at a much higher level than those bogged down by stress.

Through practicing Chi Kung, you'll be able to think more clearly and make better decisions, perform physically demanding tasks without feeling tired, work longer hours without feeling fatigue and burn out, and enjoy the entire process to its fullest even when you encounter tough obstacles and challenges.

In this book, you are going to discover more about these and other wondrous benefits Chi Kung has to offer. Then, you'll be walked step-by-step through how you can begin experiencing these benefits for yourself.

Throughout this process, you may encounter concepts and ideas that may seem strange and unfamiliar. Please, keep an open mind. Realize that Chi Kung has been developed by hundreds of great masters over the course of thousands of years and that during that time, countless tests and experiments were conducted to find the absolute best techniques and approaches for relieving stress and enhancing health.

Once you put the powers of Chi Kung to the test, like the thousands who have come before, you will experience the amazing benefits of Chi Kung firsthand. This book is simply a tool to inspire and help you do that. Try it and then make up your mind.

Keep reading, because in the next couple of hours you will discover the secrets to overcoming diseases that many consider "incurable". You will find out how to greatly reduce and even eliminate stress from your daily life, even in today's hustle and bustle fast paced environment. You'll also learn how to enhance your physical, mental and emotional health to exciting new levels even if you already consider yourself healthy.

Welcome to the wonderful world of Chi Kung!

Chapter 1:
The Wonderful Benefits
of Chi Kung

Would you believe that very serious illnesses and diseases can be permanently overcome in a matter of weeks or months? Even ones that many doctors say are incurable? And that this can be done without any pills, expensive long term treatment, or even considerable change in your lifestyle?

Many people, like you may be now, have been skeptical about the seemingly marvelous benefits of Chi Kung. But for those who have an opportunity to practice Chi Kung for themselves, as you are about to be given in this book, the skepticism becomes a short lived bump in the road as they move on to directly experience many of the amazing claims for themselves!

Like Angel, a surgical nurse who suffered from Insomnia for over 10 years. Within weeks of learning Chi Kung from me her sleep improved. Within months her insomnia was gone.

Or Lucy who gently passed dozens of kidney stones within weeks of learning Chi Kung from me. Her Medical Doctor was amazed at the result.

Julie had suffered from Migraines for years but overcame them ever since she practiced a simple and easy 15 minute daily Chi Kung exercise learned from me.

These are just some of the thousands of real life examples showing that Chi Kung is much more than just wishful thinking or a New Age practice that hasn't been carefully time tested. It is a practical and highly effective life changing exercise that puts the power to self heal, improve health and unlock an exciting new quality of life into the hands of everyday people just like you.

Before we explain how Chi Kung works, we first need to understand the scope and depth of Chi Kung's marvelous benefits.

While many exercises today have been shown to contribute considerable benefits to our physical bodies, they ultimately pale in comparison to Chi Kung's amazing transforming powers. Some people may think it is an exaggeration when they hear that Chi Kung can completely cure chronic and degenerative diseases like asthma, cancer, diabetes, rheumatism, arthritis, depression or sexual impotence. But not only is this claim true, it is confirmed by numerous case studies and scientific trials as well as the direct experiences of real people over hundreds and thousands of years. These real results are one of the main reasons that Chi Kung has been treasured and practiced by dedicated people for so long.

In general, Chi Kung's benefits can be broken up into two main categories:

The first are physical benefits. Practicing genuine Chi Kung on a daily basis enhances the functioning of literally all our body's natural systems.

Our body is built with thousands of processes that are naturally carried out to maintain our health and vitality. Most of these processes are carried out without our conscious knowledge. From digesting food to fighting off infections to carrying oxygen and other nutrients to our organs and other cells this complex system keeps us alive and functioning.

Chi Kung works to enhance these natural built in processes. either repairing processes that are "worn out" or broken, or increasing the efficiency of processes that are already giving us good health and making them even better to unlock incredible levels of health most people only dream of!

The second category is non-physical which includes mental and emotional benefits. Chi Kung is, first and foremost, a meditative exercise designed to train the mind. Besides the remarkable physical enhancements it gives a practitioner, Chi Kung offers what some may consider an even more remarkable benefit – mental, emotional and spiritual health.

If you are feeling depressed, stressed or burnt out, Chi Kung is an excellent way to regain the zestful and joyful outlook you've been missing. You will also find that with continued practice you are able to think through problems more clearly and work on mental tasks longer without becoming fatigued.

Within weeks of practice after learning from me Diego found that it was much easier to focus on the important aspects of his managerial responsibilities and not be caught up in the numerous distractions that were pressing on him thus improving his work performance. He also noticed that work associates were much more comfortable approaching and collaborating with him.

We'll dig deeper into all the ways Chi Kung will enhance your life, as well as the reasoning behind the claims in the next several chapters. In order to fully appreciate them, let's first look at a brief history of how Chi Kung came to be.

Chapter 2:
Coveted Treasures, Royal Families, And the Gathering of China's Most Brilliant Medical Minds

The Elite form of "Moving Meditation" from China's most acclaimed Monastery

Chi Kung is one of the oldest forms of exercise known to man. But don't be fooled into thinking that Chi Kung's age makes it an out dated, superstitious art. In fact, the opposite is true. Over time, Chi Kung has been meticulously and carefully refined by some of China's greatest sages and leaders.

Although Chi Kung has been practiced in the East for thousands of years a special type of Chi Kung was introduced to China about 1,500 years ago by a man named Bodhidharma who had traveled from India. Bodhidharma was no ordinary man but was in fact a great Prince, teacher and a successor to the Buddha. One day, he came to a monastery of monks at Shaolin Mountain. He found many of the monks were in poor health and lacked the energy and zest needed to pursue their spiritual quest.

To help the monks, Bodhidharma taught them a set of exercises that became known as the 18 Lohan Hands. This moving form of meditation invigorated the monks, allowing them to live long, healthy lives full of energy for all of their daily and spiritual pursuits. This marked the beginning of 1,500 years of expansion and prudent development of exercises and skills that became known as Shaolin Chi Kung.

Over the course of Shaolin Chi Kung's history, it was always kept as a jealously guarded secret. Shaolin Chi Kung not only gave its practitioners incredible health and vitality, it also gave them a competitive edge when combined with fighting arts like kung fu. While it may seem unbelievable to the uninitiated, through the practice of advanced Shaolin Chi Kung exercises warriors were able to move faster to avoid being struck, deliver more powerful blows, and, as necessary, sustain powerful hits without being harmed. In this age where your ability to defend yourself was often a life and death skill, any competitive advantages were kept strictly secret.

Beyond this, Shaolin Chi Kung was also kept secret for other reasons. Chinese royalty and other high ranking members of society were one of the few groups who had access to this incredible art. Its powers to enhance sexual performance, increase longevity and youthfulness and give the practitioner remarkable mental clarity and peace were coveted.

While many types of Chi Kung were developed and experimented with throughout China and slowly spread over the centuries, Shaolin Chi Kung stood out as the most elite of all.

To understand what sets this type of Chi Kung apart, we must take a trip back in time to the acclaimed Shaolin temple...

The Shaolin temple was named "the temple closest to heaven" and was sponsored by China's Emperors as an Imperial temple. Once a year the Emperor would travel to the Shaolin temple to pray on behalf of the people. Generals, scholars, and other members of the Chinese Empire's elite would retreat or retire to Shaolin for spiritual cultivation.

These circumstances allowed the Shaolin Temple to provide a unique environment for high level development of many Arts over the centuries. These Arts included Kung Fu, Zen and Chi Kung which are famously referred to as "The Three Treasures of Shaolin". In fact, all authentic Zen practiced around the world today can be traced directly back to the Shaolin Temple where it was also introduced by Bodhidharma who is known as the Patriarch of Zen.

Because so many Masters and Elite people were able to gather, compare, refine and develop these Arts in a methodical way for centuries the Arts were able to attain incredibly high levels of effectiveness and depth. Shaolin philosophies and principles were established and applied to all of these Arts. One example of an important principal was and still is, "Safety First". Whether in development or application of Kung Fu fighting and training or in spiritual cultivation through Zen Meditation or in Chi Kung practice the principle of "Safety First" was and still is always adhered to.

Another principle is "Simple, direct and effective" which itself is a description of Zen. This Zen principle was applied to measure all development and application of these Arts. That is, if a technique or practice, including in Shaolin Chi Kung, wasn't "Simple, direct and effective" it was either modified or discarded. The Shaolin Temple, with its incredible legacy of Masters, Wisdom and profound principles was home to the Shaolin Wahnam Chi Kung you're beginning to learn about in this book.

This gathering of great minds was a truly remarkable situation in the history of human development and medicine. China's wisest men and women came to practice and further enhance the art of Chi Kung – for physical, mental, emotional and spiritual health. Over time, subtle yet profound discoveries were made in how our mind, breathing, and other things affect our overall health and vitality.

Once a new technique was uncovered, it would be continuously tested. Only when it was clear that the new technique (or revision to an existing technique) brought concrete benefits to the practitioner in a simple, direct and effective way was it added to the repertoire.

As time went on, the Chi Kung exercises being developed at the Shaolin temple became not only more powerful, but also more time efficient for the practitioner. Results that used to take years of practice began to be achieved in a few weeks or months as the secrets of our minds and bodies were further unlocked.

So how did Shaolin Chi Kung go from a closely guarded art reserved exclusively for the most elite members of Chinese society, to being available to you now?

After the fall of the Chinese Imperial government, many of China's great Chi Kung masters left the country and began spreading across the globe. As modern conditions changed, a handful of these masters began spreading the art more generously than it had traditionally been done in the past. One of these masters was a man named Sifu Wong, the patriarch of our Shaolin Wahnam Chi Kung.

Sifu Wong is a direct successor of the Shaolin arts from the Shaolin temple. His master, Grandmaster Ho, learned from a master, Grandmaster Yang, who learned from a Chi

Kung master, the venerable Jiang Nan that had practiced and studied in the acclaimed Shaolin temple during the 19th century. Following tradition, Sifu Wong would have selected just a handful of disciples and trained them in all the wondrous Chi Kung techniques passed down to him from the Shaolin temple. However, he made several notable observations that have led to this once secret, powerful Chi Kung being available to you here today.

First, he observed that in today's modern society the Chi Kung skills previously used to defend against attackers were no longer an urgent matter of life and death. Today, having advanced fighting skills may be useful in some instances, but generally most of us do not have to worry about finding ourselves in life and death battles. Preventing these advanced Chi Kung skills from falling into the hands of an enemy that might use them against you is also not as great of a concern. Thus, the intense level of secrecy surrounding Chi Kung was also not nearly as great of a concern as it was in the past when fighting skills were more important to a person's survival.

Second, he observed the great need in the world for Chi Kung's powerful healing benefits. While conventional medicine has made incredible leaps forward in preventing and treating diseases, there are still many illnesses that have no cure. Furthermore, in today's increasingly fast paced environment, problems stemming from stress and burnout are becoming more and more common. Not only are stress related illnesses such as high blood pressure, heart disease, and insomnia a cause of serious concern for millions of people there are also a large number of people simply not experiencing the joy, excitement, and peace of mind that they were born to naturally experience.

Based on these observations, Sifu Wong made the decision to begin spreading the art and exercise of Chi Kung to as many people in need as possible. Over the past two decades, he has succeeded in helping thousands of people overcome otherwise incurable illnesses from cancer to rheumatism.

Several years ago, Sifu Wong chose me to carry on his legacy and generosity. I hope to continue the spread of these wonderful benefits with you by the end of this book.

From Emperors and Generals of Ancient China and Now Onto You

In the late 1990's I was having some serious health problems that didn't have any solutions in Western Medicine. I was a Corporate Salesmen and required to travel quite a lot. My energy and ability to do my job were reduced due to the chronic illnesses that I was suffering. I had asthma that caused me pain at times when I simply tried to breathe. This condition was typically aggravated as I tried to breathe

the cabin air on airplanes. I felt like I just couldn't get enough oxygen.

I also suffered from insomnia which only allowed me to sleep a few hours at night and significantly reduced my energy during the day.

Finally, I also experienced painful symptoms of a heart condition called Mitral Valve Prolapse (MVP). When a person has MVP the valve in their heart doesn't flush all of the blood out of the chamber which results in an often very irregular heartbeat. It can also be accompanied by pain around the heart, which I had. The condition was further complicated because the majority of the pain was on my left side, which forced me to sleep in restricted and uncomfortable positions. Believe me, if you try to restrict yourself in how you sleep it can be very frustrating.

The combined effect of all of these conditions was a lot of frustration. I had some excellent Medical Doctors but they could only offer me the conventional treatments. For Asthma I was given a spray to inhale which didn't provide any relief. For Insomnia, I was given pills that helped me sleep by making me very drowsy but I didn't really feel refreshed in the morning. For MVP, there was no known treatment. It is generally viewed as a congenital condition with no known treatment. Patients are told to accept it and live with it.

I expressed my frustration to my doctor saying, "That's it? This is what I have to live with? There's no hope?" He had some compassion, sat down next to me and told me that he had had a couple of patients over the years that had made some progress with these conditions by practicing meditation. I asked him what type of meditation but he didn't know.

It so happened that at that time I was also reading some books on Kung Fu including one about Chi Kung. The author of the book promised answers to these types of conditions by simply practicing his special style of Chi Kung.

I wrote to the master and told him about my problems. He almost laughed in his reply telling me that my problems would be overcome very quickly and easily by practicing his incredible Shaolin Chi Kung. I was desperate to find a solution to my problems and return to living a healthy, robust, normal life so in 2000 I traveled to a remote area of Malaysia to learn Shaolin Chi Kung from a Chinese Master named Grandmaster Wong.

Within months of regular practice all of my conditions disappeared never to return again. One year later an M.D. examined me and told me she couldn't believe I ever had my heart problem. Furthermore, headaches and stress related illnesses disappeared from my life never to return. Since then I've traveled frequently to Malaysia to learn and train with

Grandmaster Wong. After several years he bestowed a great honor on me by asking me to become a teacher of this amazing and rare Art in order to bring it to the United States. I did and in 2004 I began to teach individuals and groups.

I'm confident that you will have just as much success in overcoming your health problems using our incredible Shaolin Wahnam Chi Kung. I feel very privileged to be able to pass this powerful, life changing Art onto you and help you attain good health, peace and joy in your life.

Next, we'll look at where Chi Kung is today and why it is the best way to overcome illness and maintain fantastic health.

Chapter 3: From Ancient Wisdom to Modern Medicine

What Doctors and Scientists From Around the World Are Discovering About Chi Kung's Amazing Health Enhancing Power

Many people assume that if you practice Chi Kung you are completely against conventional western medicine. This is not true and in fact there are many ways that conventional medicine is more effective than Chi Kung at overcoming health problems (especially for a beginning Chi Kung practitioner). For example, if you suffered from traumatic injuries, in most cases modern surgeons would likely provide much more immediate benefit than Chi Kung. However Chi Kung would allow you to make a much faster recovery and avoid potential health complications down the road.

Immunizations and sensible use of antibiotics have proven to be of enormous value. Other modern western principles have been used to dramatically reduce infant mortality and have benefited the world a great deal.

You'll be pleased to discover that modern science continues to support what Chi Kung masters have known for centuries: that Chi Kung can and does cure virtually any physical or mental illness.

While Chi Kung has not reached a tipping point of gaining wide spread recognition in the modern medical community, there are many doctors and scientists around the world who are currently doing or have done clinical research that proves Chi Kung's remarkable ability to overcome a wide range of severe and mild health problems. Many of my own students are Medical Doctors and Nurses. They practice because they get the real benefits that Chi Kung promises.

Beyond modern clinical trials of Chi Kung's effectiveness, many of the latest medical breakthroughs in modern medicine are actually confirming what Chi Kung masters have known for hundreds of years such as our understanding that the mind is the ultimate controller of our bodily processes.

One powerful fact is the understanding that we are naturally healthy. Our body has been built with amazing and seemingly complex "systems" that fight off illness, restore cells, and maintain health all without any conscious knowledge of the person. Medical science is now developing a clearer understanding of these systems, and noting that illness only occurs when the natural built in processes of our body's fail. This is something Chi Kung masters have known for centuries, often remarking that good health is our birth right!

Keep reading to discover exactly how Chi Kung works to restore and improve these natural physical and mental systems, because in the next chapter we'll discuss the simple yet profound philosophies behind Chi Kung and give you a clear understanding of why Chi Kung is such an effective preventative and curative treatment.

Chapter 4:
Simple Direct Steps to Achieving Vibrant Health

How Chi Kung Works: *The Chinese Medicine Health Paradigm*

Chi literally translated means "energy". From the Chinese medical perspective, chi or energy exists in all things. From the chair you are sitting in, to the air you breathe, to the trees outside your window. All of these things are made up of energy. If this sounds like a silly or mystical idea, you may be interested to know that this is exactly what modern day physicists discovered when they looked at the world through high powered microscopes! At the most fundamental level, literally everything in our universe is made of energy. This was recognized and written down by Chi Kung masters in many documents thousands of years ago.

Chi Kung is the Art of Energy that taps into this fundamental source of energy, using it for our benefit. Just as we naturally take the energy from the air we breathe or extract the energy from a plate full of food – a Chi Kung practitioner taps into the good energy flowing around us all the time and harnesses it for their best benefit.

This may seem like a whimsical or imaginative concept, but let's evaluate the idea a bit further and see if it is really as strange as it may sound. In reality, human beings and other living beings tap into this same source of energy all the time – just on different levels. For example, consider how a plant converts sunlight (one form of energy) into sugars/food (another form of energy) using photosynthesis. Or, as I already mentioned, how animals and humans convert plants and meat (one form of energy) into the energy needed to fuel our cells, sustain our tissues, and give us energy to expend during our work and play.

Instead of taking energy from a source that needs to be converted (such as through digestion), Chi Kung allows us to tap into the most distilled, pure form of energy that exists. The Chinese called this type of energy "cosmic energy". Not because it is from outer space as the name sounds, but because it is the fundamental energy that makes up the cosmos, or universe.

During a Chi Kung exercise, the practitioner uses a coordination of physical movements, breathing, and mental focus to take in this pure cosmic energy.

Our bodies already have Chi flowing in them all the time from sources like food, water and the air we breathe naturally every minute. This energy flows along what the Chinese call "meridians" or energy pathways. These pathways carry the energy our body takes in to all the vital components of our body, nourishing and sustaining them.

Sometimes these energy pathways become blocked for various reasons, cutting off or limiting the flow of energy similar to how bad cholesterol restricts blood flow in your arteries. When a blockage like this occurs, the natural energy flow that is meant to sustain certain bodily functions such as your immune system, digestive system, or other key body systems is unable to deliver the nourishment these systems need to work as they were intended and unnecessary buildup of toxins occurs.

When this happens, diseases and illnesses begin to pop up in your life because your immune system was unable to function in its naturally effective way. You may find it interesting that doctors today believe we actually get cancer and other diseases literally thousands of times throughout our life. However, our body's immune systems are so effective that we never even know it – because the disease is fought off and eliminated before we experience any of the symptoms of it. So, it is only when our natural defenses fail to work as they should due to blocked energy flow that diseases like cancer, diabetes, and arthritis actually manifest into painful and life threatening symptoms.

Understanding the
Chinese Medicine Health Paradigm

Effectively Maintaining the Health and Wellness of the World's Largest and Longest Running Civilization

Chi Kung falls into the family of Traditional Chinese Medicine (TCM). This is a grouping of Traditional Chinese Medical practices that have been developed and used in China for several thousand years. You have probably heard of other practices under this umbrella such as acupuncture and herbal remedies. In order to fully grasp how Chi Kung works, it's important to understand some of the underlying philosophies of this branch of medicine.

Several thousand years ago the Chinese recognized that our physical bodies consist not just of flesh, bones and blood but also numerous energy pathways which they diagramed and recorded in famous historical texts. The Chinese established a comprehensive and effective medical system that used the recognition of these medical pathways as its basis. This system has been successfully utilized since then in a variety of treatments including Chi Kung, making it the oldest continuously used medical system in the world. Of course, over the thousands of years the system has continuously developed making it even more effective.

The Chinese Medicine Health Paradigm

The basis of this incredible Medical System is the Chinese Medicine Health Paradigm. The Chinese Health Paradigm recognizes that everything in the world is energy. We are energy. More specifically, we are a smooth flow of energy. As long as our energy flow is smooth and sufficient we are healthy. Not just physically healthy. The Chinese concept of health includes physical, mental, emotional and spiritual health. All of these four levels of health are connected.

This Chinese Health Paradigm also emphasizes harmony. When our energy flow is smooth, unblocked and sufficient it is called Yin/Yang Harmony. Thus, energy flow is sufficient and balanced throughout our body. When it isn't it is called Yin/Yang Disharmony. It is profound that in this Paradigm there is **only one illness** — Yin/Yang Disharmony. So being that there is only one illness, there is only one solution — Restoration of Yin/Yang Harmony!

Chinese Medicine has several highly developed approaches to restoring Yin/Yang Harmony. These include Acupuncture, Acupressure, Massage, Herbalism and, of course, Chi Kung. In each of these arts the therapist identifies where the energy problem is and uses a therapy to resolve it as quickly as possible. Thus, an Acupuncturist introduces needles into the patient that restore energy flow where it is needed. A similar approach is used in Acupressure and Massage. The Herbalist uses a specially balanced concoction of herbs to induce the needed energy flow and restoration as well.

Shaolin Chi Kung is the most profound of all Traditional Chinese Medicine treatments:

Incredibly, in Shaolin Chi Kung it is not necessary to know where the energy blockage is occurring in order to clear it.

How can this be? Because all of the energy meridians in the body are ultimately connected. When energy flows smoothly and with sufficient volume in the main meridians the flow eventually spreads to all of the meridians. Yin/Yang Harmony is restored and thus, health is restored. Even more profoundly, the health restored is on all levels, not just the "physical" aspect.

While acupuncture and herbal treatments aim to redirect existing Chi flow to clear out specific blockages, Chi Kung practitioners are better able to take in fresh, extra energy into their bodies and allow it to circulate. This combination of increased energy volume and holistic circulation allows the practitioner to quickly and safely break through the blockages that are causing their problems.

In the Chinese Medical Paradigm, Chi flows to where it is needed most in a natural way. This means you do not need to study TCM for years and have an intricate understanding of energy meridians in order to release the blockages that are causing your health problems. You can successfully overcome your energy blockages by simply practicing and enjoying Shaolin Chi Kung as part of your daily routine!

Shaolin Chi Kung was developed by Zen Masters over the centuries. As mentioned before, one of the three treasures of Shaolin is Zen. These were men with incredibly sharp minds which enabled them to produce a solution that transcends the typical treatments used in Chinese Medicine. Over and over again throughout history Shaolin Arts are referred to as the greatest arts. This innovation in Shaolin Chi Kung reflects this. It is simply amazing to consider that the profound Art of Shaolin Chi Kung doesn't require the Master or even the patient to know exactly where the energy blockage is in order to be successful! Knowledge of the blockage may be useful in some cases but it isn't required.

Apart from teaching people Chi Kung I provide Chi Therapy to people suffering from chronic, painful and life threatening conditions. If I know where the energy blockage is it certainly can assist me in removing it but even when I don't know the exact location success for the person receiving the therapy isn't hindered. I'm still amazed at the wisdom and generosity of the many Masters before me who developed and refined such a profound and effective system of health.

Please note that this is a general comparison between other TCM therapies and Chi Kung. This doesn't mean that other TCM therapies aren't valuable, very useful or even more appropriate for certain people. In many cases they can serve as a useful complement to Chi Kung. Acupuncture or other TCM treatments may be more suitable for certain patients. One example would be a person who is too lazy to practice Shaolin Chi Kung for 15 minutes a day or has no access to it. Acupuncture and Chi Kung can complement each other very well. Chi Kung dramatically enhances the effects of Acupuncture and herbal treatments through enhanced energy flow. There are many factors to consider but the discussion is beyond the scope of this book.

How to Restore Energy Flow for Glowing Health and Vitality!

Chinese medicine ultimately has only one cause to all our health problems: blocked or insufficient energy flow. If our meridians are clear of blockages and we have a smooth flow of energy going to all our body's systems, tissues, and other key components then we are healthy – because all these systems are getting just the right amount of energy to work perfectly. But if blockages develop and this flow of energy is unable to provide the life sustaining nourishment our system needs, then it will begin to deteriorate and cause the myriad of health problems people experience today.

Because there is only one illness, blocked energy flow, there is also one solution:
Restore energy flow. How can energy flow be restored? It is actually quite simple. In order to break through the blockages in your meridians preventing your Chi from flowing smoothly, all you need to do is safely enhance the volume of your Chi flow to allow it to circulate appropriately.

The easiest, most effective way to do this is by practicing Chi Kung. The Shaolin Chi Kung practitioner uses a combination of physical movements, breathing, and mental focus to tap cosmic energy into their body's meridian system. This extra volume of Chi into your system quickly works to push through the blockages. The "toxic" negative energy that these blockages are made up of is naturally expelled out of your body once it has been broken up and "unstuck". This ultimately results in a smoother, fuller flow of energy going to all the vital parts of your body that need it which in turn means enhanced functioning of everything in your body!

From the natural skin toning agents that keep your skin looking vibrant and healthy to your metabolism that regulates the burning of fats to the countless connections in your brain that help you think clearly, and solve problems quickly, literally every aspect of your system will be enhanced along with the energy flow that sustains it. The more smooth your energy flow is, combined with more energy that is able to flow and nourish all the different parts of your body, the more vibrant, healthy, and energized you will feel!

Another way to consider this concept of energy flow is to look at modern science's explanation of our nervous system. From this modern scientific perspective, all our body's functions are controlled by our mind. Essentially, electrical signals are sent from our brain to the various parts of our body via our nervous system with information instructing each of these parts to perform a certain task. When the nerve pathways these electrical signals are sent along become damaged or blocked, the instructions for performing certain tasks do not reach their intended destination intact – resulting in partial functioning or failure of that part of your body. Keep in mind this is simply an analogous description.

Next, we'll look specifically at how Chi Kung is used to overcome diseases. If you are suffering from any type of illness or disease, you will be excited at the possibility you now have to quickly and easily restore your health even if you have been told that your illness is "incurable" by western standards!

Chapter 5: Curing the Incurable

A New Hope for People with all Types of Diseases

You may be reading this book because you have one or more illnesses that you would like to overcome by practicing Chi Kung. As you learned in the last chapter, overcoming disease from the Chinese medical perspective is actually quite simple!

While modern medicine has made many advances in treating diseases from cancer to diabetes, in many ways their treatments are dramatically less effective than Chi Kung therapy because they don't go to the source of the problem: blocked energy flow.

We mentioned before that antibiotics are a great example of an effective treatment for many infections. One simply takes pills according to a schedule prescribed by their doctor and, voila! the infection goes away. This is wonderful. Unfortunately treatments as effective as this are not to be found for other complex conditions like diabetes, arthritis, cancer, and many more. Interestingly, a Chi Kung practitioner may never need antibiotics because their systems prevent potential infections from developing.

This is the major reason why many so called "incurable" diseases exist in the West today is because Western scientists and doctors have so far been unable to identify the true source of the problem behind the symptoms of a disease. What results is a lifelong regimen of pills and other treatments targeted at the resulting symptoms of the illness in hope of maintaining a decent quality of life for the patient.

Chi Kung is not limited in this way because its methods go straight to the source of all illnesses. With the aim of restoring energy flow, it does not matter if you have been diagnosed with life threatening cancer or simply a mild case of allergies. The Chi Kung treatment for both is virtually the same. Because once your energy flow has been restored, your body's natural systems can quickly and easily eliminate any kind of illness or disease that is attacking your body and quality of life.

While Chi Kung has been proven in countless cases to be an effective treatment on its own for even the most serious, life threatening, and debilitating illnesses we recommend that Chi Kung practitioners today take full advantage of modern medicine, as appropriate, using their own judgment in consultation with their doctor.

As your Chi Kung practice progresses, you can be weaned off of the modern medical treatments until you are fully healthy and can then rely solely on Chi Kung to continue to improve and maintain your good health into the future! This weaning should be done under the supervision of your doctor.

How quickly can Chi Kung practice help overcome your illness?

The amount of time it takes for Chi Kung to overcome your health problems depends on several factors. The first is how far the disease has already progressed. For example, if cancer has spread to many different areas of the body it will likely take longer to heal than if the cancer has just recently developed. In some rare cases, the disease may have progressed to a point where even high level Chi Kung cannot overcome it. However, if you have been told by doctors that there is no hope to live you can take heart in the fact that many patients who were only given months to live are now completely fit and healthy thanks to Chi Kung!

Another factor to consider in predicting Chi Kung's speed at overcoming health problems is underlying problems and Chi blockages you may not be aware of. Your Chi naturally flows to where it is needed most without any conscious intention or knowledge on your part. Because of this, there are many cases where it will go to work on clearing a critical blockage that may be unrelated to the illness you perceive.

In an example, a patient may have very painful arthritis and want very badly to overcome it. But there may be more important things for your Chi to work on first, such as a weak immune system or another disease you might not be aware of. Doing so, your Chi is actually helping you avoid future health complications. And you can feel confident that it will eventually get to the problems you began practicing Chi Kung to overcome in the first place. It's simply a matter of priority –your Chi will naturally flow from the highest to the lowest priority blockages.

Will Chi Kung Be Able To Cure <u>My</u> Problem?

When many people first learn about Chi Kung, they often wonder if it will help them with their unique health problem. There are literally thousands of common and not so common illnesses and variations known to man. But remember that in the Chinese Medical Paradigm there is in fact, only one illness: blocked energy flow!

Being concerned about a specific illness (or more accurately, a specific set of symptoms) is an example of only looking at your health through one perspective, that of Western medicine. If you begin to look at things from another angle, you will realize that the symptoms you are experiencing and even the things linked to them are often not the true cause of your health problems. The true cause is a failure of your natural bodily systems to maintain your health, which has occurred because of a blockage in your energy flow.

That said, can Chi Kung treat your specific problem? Absolutely yes, because it works on the underlying cause of all illnesses!

Next, we'll look at how Chi Kung treats stress related and mental illnesses. While physically disabling and life threatening illnesses can be very serious, stress related and mental illnesses can be just as much so in many ways. Keep reading to discover how you can effectively free yourself from these problems without any pills or elaborate psychological treatments.

Chapter 6: Overcoming Stress and Mental Illness

Secrets of A Clear and Peaceful Mind in Today's Stressful World

Not only is stress a daily nuisance many of us would like to avoid, it can also be much more serious and damaging. The majority of doctors agree that stress is the number one cause of illness, and the three top selling prescription drugs in the world today are for stress related problems.

Many people today are so caught up in the grips of stress that it has become something of a normal condition that they accept as an unavoidable part of life. They would indeed be amazed at just how remarkably different a life without stress could be.

When you are in a state of stress your body feels tight and uncomfortable, your mind is wrapped in a haze where sharp and quick decisions can be difficult, and you are more prone to dive into deeper negative emotions such as anger, depression, and fear.

As you begin to practice Chi Kung, you will find that stress quickly becomes a thing of the past and is replaced with a deep sense of peace and a bright new awareness of the moment. Instead of reacting to demanding situations with stress, you will feel calm, confident, and excited in the moment.

Why is this so? Unlike Western medicine which separates mental problems like stress and depression from physical illnesses, in the Chinese Medicine Health Paradigm the mind and body are closely linked. Thus, Chinese treatments are aimed at the whole person.

So, as you practice Chi Kung and clear away blockages throughout your body's energy system you not only experience improved physical health but also mental health. In fact, from the Chinese Medical perspective mental and emotional problems like stress, excessive worry, and anxiety are linked to problems in our spleen, heart, and kidneys. This may seem strange to a person used to the Western perspective that our brain is in charge of all these emotions. But if you consider that your body's entire energy system is linked together, you will see that our minds may be seriously affected by the energy flow in different parts of our body.

Another reason why Chi Kung is so effective at inducing a relaxed, confident state of mind all day long is that, first and foremost, Chi Kung works to train the mind. While the coordination of breathing and physical movements is important, the most important element of Chi Kung is the training of the mind.

Using mind training techniques that have been developed over more than a dozen centuries, you will be able to focus your mind into a relaxed, peaceful, and joyous state. As this focus develops with continued practice, the peace and joy you experience in your daily life will increase dramatically because you have trained your mind to return to its natural state of being, a state of calm and happiness.

Many people today consider that it is simply normal to feel stressed out, frustrated, and unhappy. In reality the opposite is true, Chi Kung will help you return to this natural state, so you can experience life with a wondrous new appreciation and joy for everything you do!

Next, we'll look at another common concern among many people, aging, and how Chi Kung can help you look and feel younger than you ever thought possible! While most medical treatments end once the health problem is gone, Chi Kung continues to work and unlock more and more wonderful health benefits beyond what many people consider "good health". You will soon realize that good health doesn't just mean not being sick!

Chapter 7: The Real Life Fountain of Youth

Looking and Feeling Vibrant Longer Than You Ever Thought Possible

As time passes, human beings are exposed to more harsh environmental conditions that many scientists believe are a major cause of aging, from excessive UV rays that wear down skin cells to the toxins in our food and water. With time, many of these unhealthy toxins build up in our bodies and cause increasing damage to our body and quicken the aging process as a result.

Also, for reasons scientists are still not completely sure of, there exists a breakdown of internal processes that accelerate the aging process. One popular example of this is free radicals, which are chemically reactive molecules or molecule fragments designed to attack and kill hostile foreign microorganisms. Our body naturally produces enzymes to defend our own cells against these free radicals, but as we grow older these enzymes tend to become unbalanced allowing the free radicals to run amok damaging our cells and expediting the aging process.

So why, despite these common causes of aging that we all face do Chi Kung practitioners have glowing skin, sturdy bones, flexible joints, strong muscles, and energy that lasts all day long well into their golden years?

To understand this, we must first remember that our bodies, in their natural peak state, have all the built in systems to defend against the environmental and internal "attackers". In the example of the free radicals, it is only when our natural enzyme levels become out of balance that the free radicals cause us any problems. And the buildup of poisonous and harmful toxins and dangerous radiation only occurs when our body's natural system for clearing these things away fails to perform its job correctly.

So, just as Chi Kung restores these natural processes to help practitioners overcome so called incurable diseases, it also restores the natural processes that we all have in order to clear away these potent age inducing agents.

Many scientists believe that if our genetic code, which maps out these natural systems, were the only factor in our aging process, that the average person would live to 120 years old and maintain a high quality of life up to that point. So while Chi Kung won't allow you to live forever, it will help you to live as close to the natural potential of your body as possible.

As your Chi flow is restored, the natural energy flow to age fighting systems in your body will be replenished resulting in remarkable levels of health and vitality. For a perfect illustration of this, simply look to the children in your life. A child's natural systems are running much closer to peak capacity having yet to experience the wear and tear of the years ahead. It is not the physical age that counts, but rather how well your natural systems are functioning to balance the negative outside factors pushing against your body.

Practicing Chi Kung helps you look younger and healthier to others. Nearly everyone I meet is stunned when they find out that I'm 44 years of age. Many of my students and other Chi Kung practitioners report the same thing. It is often another result that motivates people to continue their practice.

While living a long life and looking better is a wonderful aspiration, it makes little sense if you are constantly too tired to actually enjoy the time you have to live. In the next chapter, you'll discover how you can unlock an ocean of energy for your work and play that lasts all day long!

Chapter 8: An Ocean Of Energy for Work and Play

Making the Most Out Of the Time You Have –
From Run Down and Burnt Out to Steady,
Balanced Energy All Day

In today's hustle and bustle world, many people would find it wonderful to simply not feel overwhelmed, burnt out, and tired by the afternoon or early evening. And yet, Chi Kung practitioners not only do not feel overwhelmed and burnt out – they feel vibrant and full of zest all morning, all afternoon, and well into the night until it's time for bed.

Just imagine, having plenty of energy to stay focused and enjoy your work all day and then going home and feeling just as energized all night. If you're like many people, you will find that not only is it nice to simply not feel tired – but you will be able to enjoy many things you previously overlooked as well!

You will be able to accomplish more in your work, and enjoy the process of doing so from beginning to end (instead of struggling through the day feeling constantly rushed and stressed out). You'll have the energy to spend time with your family and friends instead of just laying around to catch your breath after a hard day's work. And you'll be able to pursue a variety of other enjoyable interests and hobbies that would otherwise get set aside due to lack of energy.

But more than just giving you more time, having a life full of energy improves the quality of that time. So many people today rush so quickly through their days they never stop to appreciate the beauty of life. By the time they are finally able to slow down, they're too tired and depressed to enjoy it.

By practicing Chi Kung, you'll be able to raise your energy levels so you can enjoy all your day has to offer. As you tap energy into your body during your practice, the extra energy will circulate through your meridians removing blockages in the energy flow. As these blockages are removed, more space will be available to store and circulate greater amounts of energy all day long.

In a few more chapters when you learn how to practice you'll discover how to store the extra energy you tap from the cosmos into secondary meridians, otherwise known as energy lakes. These secondary meridians hold excess energy until it is needed, so you can have a constant reserve of energy to last you all day long – no matter what kind of work or play you decide to do!

Chapter 9: Is Life Passing You By?

Immersing Yourself in the Joys of Daily Life and Taking Away More Satisfaction From Everything You Do

Most people today are so wrapped up in the "noise" of their own thoughts and the constant chatter of the world around them that they completely miss life's most wonderful experiences and sources of joy!

When was the last time you stopped to admire a glowing sunset or the swaying of trees? Or put your complete attention into the delectable taste of your daily lunch? Or lost yourself in the beautiful sounds of a symphony or favorite song or birds singing?

Too often, you probably are only half listening, or half noticing, or half tasting the world around you. In many cases, these subtle but wonderful experiences probably go completely unnoticed!

One of the greatest gifts Chi Kung has to offer is the gift of increased awareness of the moment, without the usual sense of being pulled in a dozen different directions and not fully appreciating any of them.

As you learn to focus your mind during Chi Kung practice, you will find it easier and natural to immerse yourself in the deep focus of your daily experience whether it is working on a report for work and not being distracted by the hustle and bustle of the office around you, or appreciating the beautiful surrounding on your drive home instead of getting caught up in a bunch of worried thoughts.

And as this awareness and focus is raised, so will the level of joy you take out of each of life's moments! When your mind is distracted and unfocused, it is often impossible to fully appreciate and enjoy any of the things on your mind. But when you are able to slow down the pace of your thoughts and focus on the moment at hand, you are then able to fully experience all the wonderful things about it.

This leads us to our next chapter. While it remains a taboo topic for many, it is also one of the greatest sources of joy in our daily lives. And for some, it has become mundane and even impossible to experience. Keep reading to find out how Chi Kung can put the spark back in your love life!

Chapter 10: Giving Frustrated Couples New Hope

Overcoming Sexual Dysfunction and Enhancing Your Sexual Experience

Perhaps you suffer from some form of sexual dysfunction such as erectile dysfunction or low libido. Men and women alike can feel confident that virtually all forms of sexual dysfunction can be overcome through practicing Chi Kung, even problems like infertility!

From the Chinese medical perspective sexual dysfunctions are no different than any other disease or illness and can be overcome just as the other problems we have mentioned up to this point: by breaking through blockages and restoring harmonious energy flow. As your energy flow is restored your natural functions and responses will be restored and enhanced. Practitioners of Shaolin Wahnam Chi Kung typically comment that their sexual performance is enhanced dramatically.

From the perspective of the Chinese Medical Health Paradigm a person's sexual health is a function of their overall vitality. Interestingly, from the Chinese perspective, the organ most important for vitality, thus sexual vitality, is the kidneys. Chi Kung is superb at restoring and enhancing kidney function.

Beyond overcoming sexual dysfunctions so both men and women can enjoy sex again Chi Kung can take the practitioner to new heights of sensual pleasure and performance! As your energy flow increases, so does your overall vitality. And with this increase in vitality comes more energy to have sex whenever you wish without feeling tired. While it is recommended that you enjoy a balanced sex life and do not over indulge (just as it is not good to over indulge in any activity), practicing Chi Kung will allow you to experience a rich, full sex life that many couples only dream of.

Another wonderful benefit of practicing Chi Kung is enhanced sensual awareness and sexual pleasure. Many people often make the mistake of thinking that the pleasure involved in sex comes centrally from the sexual organs. In truth, the pleasure you experience is dependent on the senses of your whole body – all of which are centered in the mind.

As you train your mind and increase your focus and ability to relax, your senses on all levels are greatly enhanced. Instead of the usual chatter going on in your mind and tendency to be distracted, you will be able to easily immerse yourself in the sensual experience of the current moment. This essentially directs all of your mind's focus into your senses. And when this happens, you will be amazed at all the subtle pleasures you have been missing!

However, a poor relationship with your partner may not be due only to sexual frustration. An exciting bonus many Chi Kung practitioners talk about is improved relationships with all the people in their life.

As stress is reduced and you begin to develop a calm, focused appreciation of the moment through your mind training, you will find that little annoyances and petty trifles quickly drift away. You soon develop a deeper sense of what is really important in life, and improve feelings of love and compassion for your friends, family, and everyone you come across throughout your day! This goes back again to our natural state of being. When we are in our natural, healthy state we do not feel hatred or aggression towards the people in our life – even when they do us wrong or make mistakes.

So, not only will Chi Kung improve your relationship in the bedroom but it will also foster a more loving, enjoyable relationship outside the bedroom as well.

Chapter 11: Overcoming All Types of Pain

Physical and non-Physical

Chi Kung has the remarkable ability to relieve all types of pain. From the minor aches and pain that people often associate with aging to the severe pain of conditions like Rheumatoid Arthritis, Migraine headaches and others. Please take a look at the Appendix of this book to see some comments from my own students on this.

If we accept that a special type of high level Chi Kung like Shaolin Wahnam Chi Kung can relieve pain one may ask how? Does is act as like an opiate and numb the pain? Chi Kung relieves pain by going to the source of the health condition that causes the pain. That is, a blockage of energy somewhere in their system. This is why the pain isn't just relieved during Chi Kung practice session which makes it different from using a medicinal painkiller. This, of course, results in a prevention of the reoccurrence of the pain that the person has suffered with.

Before I learned and practiced Chi Kung I assumed that headaches were a normal part of life as I would get at least one a week. It wasn't until after practicing for some time that

I realized that I no longer was having any headaches. I didn't learn Chi Kung to relieve headaches but it turned out to be a wonderful bonus from my practice.

All types of pain can be relieved by Chi Kung. This includes not just physical but emotional pain as well. One of the most difficult types of pain that people experience is emotional pain. Understanding the Chinese Medicine Health Paradigm explained previously allows us to realize that all illness, including the emotional, is a result of an energy blockage, insufficiency or imbalance. This explains and helps us understand why the childhood traumas that some people experience are relieved simply through high level Chi Kung. A Chi Kung master doesn't do psychiatric counseling or utilize modern methods and theories on Psychology and their associated programs in order to help people overcome their seemingly complex issues. True, the issues a person may suffer from may indeed be deep, but from the Chi Kung perspective they are not complex. They involve an imbalance of energy that has a simple solution which is to balance the energy safely. As noted in the Q & A section at the end of this book those with severe psychiatric problems typically need careful and special guidance in Chi Kung practice from a Master.

When one considers the depth and profundity of a highly developed type of Chi Kung like Shaolin Wahnam Chi Kung it truly leaves one amazed and inspired by the achievement of such a rare and special Art. This ancient, profound Art is complete and doesn't need to be, nor in most cases, should it be combined with other types of modern Western philosophies, new Psychological theories, New Age Energy Arts, etc. As explained previously, Shaolin Chi Kung is an ancient, carefully developed and refined Zen Art. This implies that it was created by Zen Masters who naturally understood and utilized Zen in their methods. Remember that Zen is simple, direct and effective. The profound and amazing Art of Shaolin Chi Kung is simple, direct and highly effective.

Chapter 12: Going To the Source
of Your Excess Weight

How to Develop a Shapely, Healthy Figure without Diets or Strenuous Exercise

Considering that the energy balancing exercises in Chi Kung improve all your body's natural systems, it makes sense that it is also an effective solution for losing excess weight and developing a shapely figure.

The Chinese medical perspective on weight loss is much different from the ideas commonly found in Western countries. From the Chi Kung point of view, vigorous exercise like aerobics and jogging are not recommended because they waste too much energy, and often result in the practitioner becoming over weight again if they ever quit the exercise. In the Chinese Medicine Health Paradigm, forcefully burning protein and carbohydrates is not only unnatural but also unhealthy.

Similarly, severe dieting is also viewed as harmful because it restricts necessary energy for your work and play. And it can lead to nutrient and energy deficits for important bodily functions, such as the immune system for fighting disease.

For an example of why some of these views are flawed, you don't need to look far. You probably know of a few people who are quite thin, and yet eat as much as they like whenever they want. And you probably also know a few people who are very careful about what they eat and only eat small quantities, and yet remain considerably overweight. This is due to natural body systems not functioning as they are intended to, such as an imbalance of hormones that regulate the burning and processing of fat.

Through the practice of Chi Kung, these natural systems can be restored to function properly and the right amount of hormones will be produced to regulate your weight down to a healthy level (or allow you to gain weight if you are very skinny). Your Chi Kung practice will guide you to your ideal, healthy weight naturally.

In the same way, the natural bodily systems that control when your body needs more energy and makes you feel hungry will also be regulated. So if you have a problem with constantly craving food, these cravings will also become balanced and make it so you are only hungry when your body actually needs to eat.

The difference between the Chinese Medicine approach to overcoming weight problems and the Western approach is a good example of treating the symptom and not the root cause.

In the Western approach, people aggressively exercise and diet to try to eliminate the excess fat in their stomachs, hips, and arms. However, the excess fat is actually only the symptom of a deeper underlying cause. In this case, the root cause is an imbalance of hormones and other natural systems in our body that regulate weight and appetite. Through the practice of Chi Kung, these natural systems can be restored to full efficiency. And once the root cause has been taken care of, the symptom of unsightly excess weight easily disappears!

Chapter 13: Unlocking Creativity and Better Decision Making for Professionals

How Artists can Unlock Creativity and how Executives can improve their Decision Making and Problem Solving

The benefits of Chi Kung practice extend to both artists, businesspeople, managers and executives.

After a Chi Kung practice session during a class I will sometimes ask my students, many of whom are Senior Executives, if they can see how our practice helps workplace productivity and improved decision making. These would be classes where the stated objective is general improvement of their welfare and not explicitly Business Improvement classes which I conduct as well. They always answer that it is obvious to them. They answer this way because of the mental and emotional state they are in after our practice not because they consider other factors like reduced absenteeism due to illness or improved morale. The students answer this way because it is intuitive to them because in their current state of mind they realize they can quite easily perform at a high level. This state of mind is relaxed and confident.

Most trained executives are very talented people with a lot of experience in their fields. When their performance is reduced it is typically because they are stressed due to the immense pressures they are under. However, when they are in a relaxed, confident and clear state of mind they can more easily discard distracting thoughts and pressures and focus on the most productive and effective approaches and tasks that their organizations need.

Mental, intellectual and creative work requires more energy than physical work. When someone is tired, especially mentally, it is difficult to perform any kind of productive work. Just trying to get by is not the same as excellent performance. Of course, Chi Kung is an energy art so one can realize how useful it is. Better yet, you can experience it when you learn to practice successfully. You may even experience this very soon after you practice as described in a later chapter of this book.

Often when creative people aren't productive it is because they feel and say that they are blocked. The concept of writer's block is generally understood by those that have suffered from it. Remember that according to the health paradigm that I previously explained when a person is healthy and functioning at their peak it is because their energy is flowing well and not blocked. Also recall that according to this paradigm all four levels of health, physical, mental, emotional and spiritual are connected. From this viewpoint, a traditional Chinese viewpoint, they cannot be disconnected and unrelated. Our Chi Kung practice provides healthy functioning on all four levels, whether we may immediately realize it or not. This gives us a perspective on how it helps our mental functioning.

Artists and creative people already have developed and refined their artistic skills. They have practiced their guitar, drawing abilities or whatever their talent is. At this point they simply need to let the creativity flow to either express musical vision or use their skills to create the unique and inspiring expression that their clients need for their marketing needs as two examples. Chi Kung practice allows them to have the relaxed, creative mindset they need to perform successfully. Keep in mind that Shaolin Wahnam Chi Kung is a Zen art. My own teacher has explained how the greatest achievements in Arts and Sciences were attained while the respective people were in a Zen state of mind, whether they knew it or not. Their minds were clear and their emotional states confident and inspired so they could transcend the typical and attain the extraordinary. The results of a profound Zen practice are never ordinary.

Writing a book may seem like a daunting task to some people. Writing this book is easy for me for several reasons. One, I'm an expert in the field. I don't have to do any research to present the concepts because I know them intuitively through my years of practice and experience. Another is that I can operate in a relaxed Chi Kung state of mind which allows me to have a mind clear of confusion on what and how to present the concepts. My goal in this book is to inspire readers, avoid wordiness and present the concepts simply, directly and effectively. Although I certainly wouldn't declare this a perfect book I'm confident that I'm achieving this, especially due to the response from the first edition published.

Open Heart = Open Mind

One further relevant concept that can help our understanding is that of open heart = open mind. Our profound Shaolin Chi Kung practice opens our heart figuratively. What we in the West consider the heart is understood from the traditional Chinese perspective as heart/mind. Shaolin Wahnam Chi Kung practice opens our hearts which provides many benefits. First, the heart is considered the Emperor Organ from the Chinese point of view. Thus, all systems are connected and benefit from a healthy functioning heart. But more relevant here is that as our heart opens our mind opens. We have the ability, mindset and energy to have intellectual and creative curiosity and expression. Conversely a person with a closed heart/mind will lack enthusiasm and curiosity or the vigor needed to learn, experience and implement new and helpful things for their life. A person with a closed heart will be closed to love as well, but that is for another publication that you can look forward to.

I learned this concept of open heart = open mind not through reading about it beforehand or after but from direct experience which is an example of a result of Zen practice. The direct experience came first and the intellectual understanding and explanation followed.

Chapter 14: Peak Athletic Performance

Helping Athletes Outperform the Competition

Athletes need glowing health and reduced stress just like everyone else and can benefit immensely from the multi-faceted benefits of Chi Kung practice. These benefits include increased energy and power, rapid recovery from injuries, reduced stress, balanced emotions and a clear mind. At the highest levels of Athletics often a small improvement or adjustment can be the difference in winning and defeating the competition. Certainly an improvement in any and certainly all of these areas mentioned above can provide a significant advantage for the Chi Kung practitioner.

Chi Kung is an energy art and couldn't even be called Chi Kung if it didn't improve a person's energy. Due to the demanding schedules, travel and training programs of today's Professional and Amateur Athletes more energy would always be welcome. Many athletic competitions themselves are grueling and when a performer can draw on more energy than their opponents at the end of a match they give themselves a dramatic advantage. More energy also allows them to conduct their training in a more productive manner. With more energy it is easier for them to focus on and perfect their form and strategies as needed and not be struggling just to practice or train.

Another influential factor in athletic performance is how one recovers from injuries. Both the speed and quality of the recovery are important. Again, Chi Kung is renowned for providing stunningly rapid and thorough recovery from injuries. Over time, as an Athlete gains skill in their consistent practice of a high level style of Chi Kung like Shaolin Wahnam Chi Kung their entire system will be enhanced which will help prevent and minimize future injuries as well.

Today's athletes are not immune to stress and often are subject to more stress due to the many demands placed upon them. We've spent some time in this book on how stress is reduced and what its benefits are from Chi Kung practice so it is easy to see that an Athlete can benefit from this. Also they can easily integrate this into their daily training. As one will read in a later chapter on practice it is easy to add one or two 15 minute practice sessions to anyone's daily schedule. An athlete may naturally desire benefits beyond stress relief so their program may include other Chi Kung practice to obtain other benefits as noted above, especially more power and stamina. There are many techniques in Shaolin Chi Kung renowned for providing powerful results but they should be carefully trained under a qualified Master.

Balanced emotions are just as important for Athletes as they are for everyone else. Although emotion can play a positive role in Athletic competition it can work as a disadvantage when not managed properly. Team and Individual Sports Managers often recognize the importance of this but typically lack effective tools to help their personnel. Both in their professional as well as personal lives Athletes need healthy, balanced emotions. We have previously explained how this is intrinsic in high level Chi Kung practice like Shaolin Chi Kung because the effects work on the physical, mental, emotional and spiritual simultaneously.

Finally, and perhaps most importantly, Chi Kung is high level mind training. Shaolin Wahnam Chi Kung is a Zen art. Often athletes will comment how they "were in a zone" when they performed their best. They comment on how the game "slows down" when they are in "the zone" and they can easily see their opponent's movements and make the best decisions on how to respond. Many athletes have been in "the zone" but find it elusive to get back into this state. When one practices Shaolin Wahnam Chi Kung they find that getting into "the zone", which we call "a Chi Kung State of Mind", is easy because it is practiced every day. This is surely another Wonder of Chi Kung.

When we consider again that the legendary Shaolin Arts are referred to in Chinese Classical literature as "the best" it is easy to see how they can give today's athlete a significant edge over the competition.

Chapter 15: Practicing High Level
Chi Kung

Advice to Help you Avoid Mistakes and Ensure you get the Best Results

Now that you have a good perspective of how Chi Kung works and the wonderful possibilities it holds for you, whatever your health problems or aspirations may be, it's time to consider what type of Chi Kung that you should begin practicing to get effective results.

There are many different Chi Kung schools around the world, offering hundreds of different "types" of Chi Kung. So which one is right for you? In choosing a Chi Kung school, there are several very important criteria to consider.

First, consider the authenticity and lineage of the Chi Kung being taught. Today Chi Kung has become a wide spread and popular way to reduce stress and increase health. However, in its popularity Chi Kung has also become extremely diluted and in many cases ineffective. This is due to a break down in the traditional means of passing on the subtle skills and knowledge for effective Chi Kung practice from one generation to the next.

Direct, heart to heart transmission of skills is the practice and tradition of Shaolin. This means an accomplished Shaolin Master passes on the skills of effective practice to a student personally.

In the past, masters were extremely selective about whom they chose to pass on their Chi Kung wisdom and skills to. This was in great part due to the fact that many centuries ago advanced Chi Kung skills gave practitioners incredible advantages in surviving the harsh, sometimes barbaric environment, from being able to maintain a high level of energy in battle and to maintain focus when matching wits with an enemy, to surviving when food was not plentiful. Another key reason for this careful selection was the commitment needed by students in order to truly acquire the essence of the Chi Kung art form. Masters intended their hard work and insights to survive for many generations, and knew that in order for this to happen they must only accept students who would be willing to study and practice the lessons they had to share with the dedication necessary for truly grasping the deep wisdom involved.

This careful selection process has meant that an incredible wealth of experience and wisdom has remained intact for thousands of years. But today, this process is the exception and not the norm. Many practitioners today will learn from a book and proceed to open up a local class and teach what they have learned to members of their community. Others may take a class or seminar and deem themselves competent to instruct others before they themselves have even mastered the art and learned deep, profound aspects of it that come only with dedicated practice over time. In the process, they have inadvertently begun transferring degraded and oftentimes outright false information to others due to their inexperience and ignorance. As this cycle of inexperienced teachers continues on, the once powerful and elite art of Chi Kung quickly becomes just a form of gentle physical exercise with comparatively limited benefits and sometimes harmful side effects, even if not intentional. Furthermore, the self appointed or inexperienced teacher is unable to properly identify and correct improper practice which is another significant disservice to his students.

A lineage is simply a line of masters that have succeeded one another over time or the master of the master and so on. If, like in the example above, you discover that the "master" of a teacher you are interested in learning Chi Kung from is actually a book then you will probably want to search elsewhere for someone who has at least learned Chi Kung from a real live person (this is important because there are many subtle elements that cannot be taught or detected through a book).

The next important thing to look for is what kind of training the master or teacher has received. This can be found by simply asking the instructor. If he has only been learning and practicing Chi Kung himself for a few months it is probably a good bet that he has not developed the high level of skills and understanding for effectively and safely transmitting the art to new students.

The last and probably most important factor to consider is whether or not the master embodies the benefits you have learned about in this book. To a trained person, like you are becoming, spotting a master is actually quite easy. He must, first and foremost, be in excellent health himself. If he has practiced Chi Kung for years and still suffers from some severe health problems it is unlikely that he or she has been practicing genuine, high level Chi Kung. He will have good posture. One shoulder won't be lower than the other. He won't have any kind of hunch in his back. He will look balanced and healthy. His face and eyes will be symmetric and balanced. One eye or socket won't be smaller than the other. His skin will look healthy and his muscles rounded. You will also be able to spot a master by his or her presence. He will be calm and relaxed, yet exude a wonderful joy and happiness that is easy to detect. He won't be aggressive as some Martial Artists become after improperly practicing Chi Kung. One good sign of a master is the bright sparkle of his eyes.

He will also be healthy mentally and emotionally. He will exhibit discretion and wisdom in his communications with students. He or she won't be spouting New Age theories and ideas or other philosophies most of which he or she is confused about and cannot communicate clearly and intelligently. He or she won't be trying to combine Chi Kung with other of these philosophies which would reflect that this "teacher" doesn't even understand the depth and wisdom of Chi Kung in the first place. A competent teacher with integrity won't try to mystify the Art for some purpose. He or she will be emotionally stable and not easily irritable or manic in their behavior.

Reading this book is a great first step toward practicing genuine, high level Chi Kung. Shaolin Wahnam Chi Kung does not come from the fanciful imagination of someone who read a book or purchased a DVD, but from a long line of some of the highest level masters in history.

Shaolin Chi Kung was first conceived at the acclaimed Shaolin temple in China over 1,500 years ago. Until the destruction of the temple, this powerful style of Chi Kung was honed and developed for centuries by some of the wisest men and women in China.

To understand Shaolin Chi Kung's origins, we first need to understand the origins and history of the Shaolin Temple in which it was developed. As mentioned earlier in this book the Shaolin Temple was a monastery high in China's central mountains. During its early years, it was visited by many travelers. One day, a very special man named Bodhidharma visited the monks after traveling from India. He noticed that the monks, despite their dedicated pursuit of spiritual fulfillment, were often tired and would fall asleep during their meditation. To help them, he taught them a powerful set of exercises. These Chi Kung exercises practiced at the Shaolin Temple became known as the 18 Lohan Hands and gave the monks incredible health and vitality.

Over time, the monks continued to practice and refine these original Chi Kung exercises. Over the centuries, the experiences and insights of the monks were used to expand and develop Chi Kung exercises that were even more powerful and efficient than before. The Shaolin Temple soon became known as the epicenter of Chi Kung development throughout China, and began to attract China's greatest scholars and warriors. It was the Imperial temple for China, the temple in which the Emperor and other powerful figures would come to pray on behalf of China's people.

The Shaolin Temple became a place of physical, mental, and spiritual practice and development for the most elite members of Chinese society and up to the period of its destruction by warring factions in China, it cultivated the art of Chi Kung to an incredibly high level – both in terms of positive results for the practitioner and the efficiency and time in which those results could be achieved.

After its destruction some of the monks were able to escape and continue to practice Chi Kung outside of the temple walls. Of these, two monks named Zhi Shan (Chee Seen) and Jiang Nan (Kong Nam) continued the legacy of Chi Kung, passing on their arts to a small handful of deserving students. As a reader of this book, you are lucky to be able to receive the wisdom of both of these monks!

My teacher, Sifu Wong Kiew Kit is fortunate enough to be a direct successor of both of these monks' teachings through his two teachers, Sifu Ho Fatt Nam and Sifu Lai Chin Wah. What a blessing to have come across not just one teacher whose lineage could be directly traced back to the acclaimed Shaolin temple but two! Our school received its Wahnam name to honor these great masters.

This powerful art is now being passed onto you. Without the intention of sounding conceited or arrogant, this is a rare honor and privilege in the scope of Chi Kung's history. In the past, students often had to beg a master to share this art with them or go through rigorous trials to prove their worthiness for months or years on end. While modern times call for different measures as we've discussed previously in this book, it is still useful to consider the extent in the past that students went to discover these teachings.

As a practitioner of Shaolin Wahnam Chi Kung, you will enjoy much higher results in a much quicker time frame than Chi Kung available elsewhere today because what you will be practicing is genuine Chi Kung with all the insights and wisdom of some of the greatest masters still intact.

Chapter 16: Little-Known Secrets for High Level Results

What many "Masters" Leave Out

Now, it's time to begin laying the foundation for the actual skill of practicing high level Chi Kung. While there are many subtle keys to getting the most out of your practice, the following are some of the most important principles to keep in mind in order to achieve high level results in minimum time.

One. High level Chi Kung is **simple and profound**.

In many things in life, people make the mistake of thinking that the more complex something is, the more advanced and effective it will be. In Chi Kung, complexity does not equal better. Some Chi Kung styles incorporate incredibly elaborate visualizations of wonderful colors of energy flowing into and around your body as well as a multitude of different steps to successfully complete the exercise.

Shaolin Wahnam Chi Kung has been refined over generations to eliminate all unnecessary steps and elements, resulting in an incredibly simple but extremely effective and profound combination of physical movements, breathing, and mental focus. This reflects the

Shaolin, and thus Zen, principle that we discussed earlier of "Simple, direct and effective".

It's very important that as you begin to learn these exercises you don't unnecessarily complicate a simple task. Many beginners will inadvertently harm themselves and greatly limit their results by adding or changing what has been developed by hundreds of masters over 1,500 years. You can rest assured that throughout the development of Shaolin Wahnam Chi Kung, the ideas you come up with for improving the exercise have very likely already been thought of and thoroughly tested by many other masters. If something is a part of the exercise, it is because it works. And the same reason goes for something not being part of the exercise.

Your job is very simple. Follow the easy directions and enjoy yourself!

Two. Realize that you practice a "**meditative exercise**".

While the physical movements and breathing are important aspects of Chi Kung, by far the most important of all is the mind aspect. Chi Kung training works to gently train your mind to attain a relaxed state. Things like worries, frustrations, and everyday mental "chatter" are gently let go of to attain a joyful awareness of the moment and nothing else. Thus, our meditative exercise doesn't involve listening to music as we practice or mindlessly doing physical techniques while we watch a television.

A common problem beginner's face is avoiding intellectualization about how Chi Kung works, what your Chi is doing, and why Chi does what it does. The reason this is so detrimental is because it gets in the way of the important process of letting go of your thoughts during your practice and often also leads to over complicating your practice like we have discussed above.

It's important to keep in mind that not only have the Chi Kung exercises themselves been meticulously refined over the long line of masters, the methods for transmitting and teaching the skills necessary for practicing Chi Kung have also been developed and refined to a very high level. If an explanation of a certain direction or point will help you develop the skills more effectively, it will be included. If an explanation will not be helpful at that point in your development, it will be left out.

Again, your job is very simple. Just follow the instructions and enjoy yourself! Over time, as your training progresses, you will come to understand Chi Kung not from an intellectual standpoint but from personal, direct experience.

Three. Practice **consistently and safely**.

Practice consistently and safely as you've been taught by your Instructor and you can expect successful results. This would seem obvious but amazingly it can get ignored or not adhered to for one reason or another.

Chi Kung is certainly safe, as long as it is practiced according to the guidelines provided by your instructor. This is reasonable when one considers that Chi Kung is an energy art. Different types of Chi Kung may be practiced very differently and utilize different guidelines. One type of Chi Kung may be practiced in a way that wouldn't be appropriate for another type of Chi Kung.

A high level energy art like Shaolin Wahnam Chi Kung is able to obtain fantastic results by practicing daily for 15 minutes because it is powerful. It is also safe as long as the simple guidelines are followed. Another type of Chi Kung that involves 2 one hour sessions per day may require different guidelines because the level of result (in this case probably a lower level because it takes so much practice to achieve results) and the aims of the exercises may be different.

Shaolin Wahnam is a high level and elite type of Shaolin Chi Kung that has several guidelines for practice. Remember, "safety first" is an important Shaolin principle, thus, the masters passed down many useful guidelines to us so that we can avoid unwanted results in our practice.

Shaolin Wahnam Chi Kung is practiced each day before 9 am and after 5 pm. We avoid practicing in the middle of the day. We practice no more than twice a day unless specifically advised by our instructor who is familiar with our particular circumstances. It is advised to practice in an open, safe area and not on a balcony or an area like next to a cliff. We practice in a clean area and not one with strong unpleasant odors. We avoid practicing in direct sunlight, shade is best. We also avoid practicing near cemeteries because the energy there isn't good for us. We wear shoes when we practice and women should avoid high heels during the practice. Finally, we also avoid practice in the midst of a lightning storm.

The most important factor is to practice in a proper state of mind which infers that you don't practice in a wrong state of mind. This is something that is best demonstrated and transmitted to you when you learn directly from an instructor. Put simply though, don't practice when you are in an agitated or angry state of mind.

Another factor that can inhibit good results is carrying on an adverse lifestyle. One may practice correctly, consistently and safely yet at the same time carry on a lifestyle of frequent excessive drinking, sleep deprivation and excessive sex, for example, and find that they aren't seeing positive results from their practice. You may chuckle to yourself when I mention excessive sex. Admittedly I've heard more than a few people mention that they have trouble getting "enough" sex. However I simply mention it as an example, albeit for many, a remote one. This would make sense because the energy demands of their lifestyle exceed the energy that they are taking in from their correct Chi Kung practice. As long as one conducts a normal lifestyle with some exceptions for certain events that demand more energy, like having to work all night on occasion, one may expect to achieve success in their Chi Kung practice. After all, high level and elite Chi Kung like Shaolin Wahnam Chi Kung allows one to do more in life than one normally could. If you need to overcome a significant illness it would be recommended that you conduct a moderate lifestyle until your Chi Kung practice overcomes the condition. After you achieve this you can move forward in life enjoying whatever you like. Later if you need to work longer hours, for example, you will be able to with plenty of zest and a happy disposition.

Chapter 17: Beginning Your Practice

Lifting the Sky for Incredible Health and Vitality

As we discussed in the last chapter, more is not necessarily better in the world of high level Chi Kung like Shaolin Wahnam which is why to start you off on your journey into the wonderful and exciting world of Chi Kung, I am going to teach you one exercise. But don't be fooled...

High level health benefits are not achieved by knowing lots of exercises and techniques. Many students and so-called "masters" spend many years acquiring lots of knowledge of the many different Chi Kung exercises. Yet, even after many years they still become tired easily, get sick often and are irritated easily. Is this because the exercises they have learned are not effective? Not necessarily. It is because they have not practiced these exercises with the depth of skill required to attain high level results.

Just like many other art forms, there is a very big difference between having a lot of knowledge about something and having a lot of skill in something. One requires only spending time learning, while the other requires practice. For example, someone may know a lot of recipes from reading many cookbooks. But if they have never been in a kitchen and applied them, they will not know the many subtleties to creating a delicious meal. In other words, they do not have the skill of a great chef even though they know a lot about cooking.

In order to help you begin developing the skills that will allow you to unlock vibrant health and vitality, it is best to focus on only a few exercises in the beginning so you can immerse yourself deeply into them rather than only skimming the surface of many different exercises.

The exercise you will learn here is called Lifting the Sky. You may be amazed to hear that just by practicing this one simple exercise you can overcome virtually any disease, greatly reduce stress, boost energy levels, and enjoy a happier disposition all day long. For many of my students, this is the reason why Lifting the Sky is the number one choice in their daily Chi Kung practice. It is an extremely effective and enjoyable Chi Kung pattern.

Even though direct and personal heart to heart transmission of skills is most effective, be confident that you can still get good results by practicing as instructed in this book. When you get the opportunity to learn from a competent instructor in person you will experience the difference and be able to get greater and more profound results.

Lifting the Sky: Step-By-Step

Simply follow the directions without adding or subtracting anything.

▶ Stand upright with your feet fairly close together as in the picture above.

▶ Let your arms hang naturally at your sides.

▶ Loosen your knees so they aren't locked.

▶ Close your eyes.

▶ Open your mouth and breathe naturally. Keep your mouth open throughout the practice session.

▶ Smile from your heart.

▶ Feel your whole body relaxed with no tension anywhere. Take your time to feel relaxed. You can take from a few seconds to a few minutes.

▶ Now place your relaxed hands and arms in the ready position as viewed in the picture above.

▶ Raise your arms smoothly as your breath in gently.

▶ Your eyes are closed but your face and eyes follow your hands from the ready position upward to the apex.

► At the apex above your head, pause in your breath and movement. Gently press up then lower your arms smoothly as you exhale gently with your mouth open.

►Your face returns to face forward as your arms drop.

▶ Repeat this pattern as described above 20 to 30 times. Enjoy the rhythm of the patterns.

▶ After you have completed 20 to 30 repetitions let your arms drop to your sides, spread your legs out to shoulder width or more. With your eyes remaining closed enjoy the peaceful state you are in and enjoy the energy flow. If your body wants to move, don't resist and follow the movements. If your body doesn't move, have no worries and simply enjoy the peaceful state.

▶ After 5 or 10 minutes, gently think of your lower abdomen for a few seconds.

▶ Gently slow your movements and bring them to a stop as you bring your feet back together and stand upright again.

▶ After you've stopped moving enjoy the stillness for as long as you like. This can be from 10 seconds to a minute or two.

▶ To complete, rub your hands together in front of you and then massage your face, scalp, ears and neck. Rub your hands together again and gently dab your palms on your eyes as you slowly open them.

▶ Walk about 30 steps briskly.

▶ Enjoy the rest of your day or evening!

Chapter 18: The Path toward Outstanding Health and Vitality

Important Reminders for Your Journey into the World of Chi Kung

I hope this book has helped give you a glimpse into the many wonders of Chi Kung and inspired you to explore the marvelous benefits it has to offer for yourself.

The next step on the path to achieving the remarkable levels of health and vitality you seek is to make Chi Kung a part of your daily routine and practice, practice, practice.

It is good to have a clear, reasonable goal of why you want to practice Chi Kung and what you want to achieve. Write it down and place it in a drawer so you can evaluate and confirm your attainment at a later time.

It is important not to grasp too tightly at the end results you seek. Chi Kung is a form of mind training, and a big part of that training is learning to let go and simply enjoy the wonderful unfolding of life and the moment. If you become too eager for the goals you are aiming to achieve with your practice, it can get in the way of this process of letting go and as a result actually impede your progress. Thus, it is advised that you don't spend every day checking to see if your condition has disappeared. Simply enjoy your practice and don't dwell on your condition. Periodically, perhaps every 6 weeks or so, take out your paper and evaluate your progress.

Keep in mind that your Chi naturally knows where to flow and will go to work to relieve the blockages in your energy flow that are causing the most serious damage to your health. While you may be very eager to overcome a certain disease, enjoy a better sex life, have energy that lasts all day, or a wide range of other objectives – keep in mind that these goals will be achieved in the order of importance to your overall health. There may be a more serious problem Chi Kung needs to address first before dealing with the things you think are most urgent. Reducing stress is typically a high priority issue that your enhanced Chi flow will address fairly quickly. It will also improve with time.

The best thing to do is simply step back and enjoy the process with the gentle awareness that each day you are becoming healthier and healthier and that with continued practice, all your health goals will be achieved and that in the process, you may have avoided other health problems that you weren't even aware of.

From the Shaolin perspective absence of illness isn't health. One must have a zest for life with joy and a twinkle in the eye.

Chi Kung is a lifetime form of health maintenance, health improvement, and disease prevention. It is not something that you practice for a few weeks to get what you want and then quit. To keep your energy pathways clear and smooth, abundant energy flowing to all your body's systems for optimal health you must practice Chi Kung every day. If you quit your practice, blockages in this energy flow may develop and poor health may return.

However, daily practice will not be a burden. This is simply because Shaolin Wahnam Chi Kung is so enjoyable! Look at your daily practice session as a short, 10 to 15 minute part of your day where you take some time to relax and let go of the hustle and bustle around you. As you begin to develop the skills to relax, let go and enjoy yourself, you will find that your daily practice is something that you don't want to miss. Each session will be a calming, deeply refreshing part of your day.

So, let go and enjoy yourself! Watch as your health is transformed with this wonderful art. I hope to meet you in person someday soon, and celebrate the exciting new levels of vitality, energy, health, peace, and joy you have unlocked through your practice.

Chapter 19: Meditation or Exercise?

Shaolin Chi Kung- A Gentle, Meditative Exercise

I often describe the Shaolin Wahnam Chi Kung that we practice and teach as a "gentle, meditative exercise". We can say exercise because there are bodily movements. We say meditative because we are in a meditative state of mind when we practice. Gentle because the movements, breathing and meditation are gentle.

Interestingly we don't set out to meditate when we practice. We simply relax and practice the movements and breathing and enjoy our Chi Kung. As we practice we find we are in a meditative state of mind. What does meditative state of mind mean? As is typical in Chi Kung, descriptions are somewhat poor substitutes for actual experience but it means, amongst other things,-

• We aren't in an agitated state of mind. We are relaxed.

• We aren't thinking about "problems" at work or other concerns elsewhere. Even if a thought can come up about a "problem" we simply note it and "throw it away".

- We feel deep pleasure and peace.

- We are focused. The focus is on the pleasure of the practice itself.

- Our awareness is heightened. Without trying we notice things nearby that we may not have noted in our typical day to day mindset when we may be rushing about. Things like birds singing and the subtle, beautiful scent of flowers and plants we haven't noticed before. (with practice our awareness is heightened even when we are aren't formally practicing Chi Kung)

Our meditation isn't forced and, because of the profound development by generations of Shaolin Masters, it is accomplished easily. We don't ever have to think of it as meditation. Shaolin Masters weren't and aren't concerned with analyzing whether we are meditating or not. The measure of a Shaolin Art is if it is effective and that is the Master's concern.

We also may call it an exercise because we use movements. An observer may think it is simple stretching and rotation of limbs. However, we don't breathe hard and our breath rate doesn't go up as we practice as most people would associate with physical exercise. The purpose of the movements isn't physical. It is energetic. It is to open up energy channels and facilitate a smooth flow of energy in an effective way. The physical movements accomplish this. Their purpose isn't to strain muscles in order to generate a muscular result.

Finally the Shaolin Chi Kung that we teach is gentle in all respects. The meditation, as explained above, is gentle and not forced. The movements and associated breathing patterns are gentle. All of the patterns and techniques that we teach in our classes and seminars are gentle. There are some Shaolin Chi Kung practices that aren't as gentle and can even be forceful but that are only taught to certain students under careful supervision as needed to accomplish a particular goal.

So we can say that the Shaolin Chi Kung that our students enjoy is a gentle, meditative exercise. But what does it accomplish? It brings pleasure and other benefits both during the session and in our everyday lives. When one considers the seemingly countless health benefits that Shaolin Chi Kung provides like relieving stress, overcoming numerous chronic illnesses and preventing illnesses and improving ones energy one can certainly say that it is profound. However one must practice it to really appreciate its profundity. Our students typically begin to appreciate the profundity during their first training session with us if not within a very short time. Over time, as students see remarkable improvements in their life, they may never stop marveling at the profound depth of this "gentle, meditative, exercise"

Some Answers to Frequently Asked Questions

Q: Does one need to face in a certain direction to practice Qigong?

A: It is true that facing east is best but there are other factors to consider. For example, if facing east requires you to stand a few feet away from and facing a wall then facing east wouldn't be best. It would be better to face toward an open area. You should follow the guidelines of the type of Chi Kung that you practice. In some types of Chi Kung it is important to face east. This can be because the extra benefit of facing east is necessary to help get results. In a high level type of Chi Kung like Shaolin Wahnam Chi Kung not facing east isn't a hindrance.

Q: Are there any dietary restrictions for practicing Chi Kung?

A: As stated previously you should follow the guidelines of the style of Chi Kung that you practice. In a high level Chi Kung like Shaolin Wahnam Chi Kung there are no dietary restrictions of any kind.

Q: Can someone with a mental illness practice Chi Kung?

A: Yes, but if someone has a severe emotional problem or mental illness they need to be personally taught by a competent instructor. It is likely that the Chi Kung will need to be modified to suit the person's unique condition.

Q: Can children practice Chi Kung?

A: Yes, but they usually should be taught at a lower level than adults. A competent instructor will be able to provide useful guidance to them. Although there is a science to Chi Kung which makes use of the Chinese Medicine Health Paradigm the instruction and practice of Chi Kung is an Art. This is why a competent instructor is essential in order to obtain great results in a safe manner.

Q: Are there any signs to watch for that help me know if I'm practicing Chi Kung correctly?

A: Certainly! You should feel refreshed after your practice, no matter how you were feeling before you practiced. If you don't feel refreshed something is wrong with your practice. What is wrong could be any number of things that are too numerous to list. This is another reason that people should practice under the guidance of a Master. They can consult with the Master as necessary.

Q: What will I experience during a practice session of Chi Kung?

A: You will feel very relaxed and at peace. You may experience sensations like warmth or tingling in your hands or feet or in other parts of your body. Your body may sway gently or at times vigorously. You may not move at all but you will feel a profound stillness that is pleasurable. What is important is that you enjoy yourself and leave behind concerns and worries about what you may experience. It is counterproductive to critically analyze your experience or results each time you practice. Just enjoy the practice and the results like overcoming illnesses will take care of themselves before too long.

Q: Do I have to avoid eating or doing anything else before or after my daily 15 minute practice?

A: Allow yourself 15 to 30 minutes after your practice before you take a shower. You may take a shower right before your practice. Also, try to wait about 30 minutes or so before making love. This will allow the Chi that you have generated in your session to "settle" and not be drained away. If you can't wait to make love then go right ahead and enjoy yourself. Just be aware of this consideration in terms of your regular, daily practice. As for eating, one may eat right before or after their practice in our style of Chi Kung.

Q: I've been practicing for several weeks now since learning from you and I've noticed that I've been passing a bit of gas recently. Is this normal?

A: Please keep in mind that as you progress in your practice your body will experience cleansing as toxins are gently flushed out of your body. Temporary passing of gas or bad breath are just that, temporary, as your body cleanses. You are experiencing a remarkable and natural detoxification. You're doing well so carry on!

Q: Can Chi Kung help people with addictions?

A: Yes, of course. In fact in can be the most powerful factor in allowing people to overcome their addictions.   An addiction represents an energy blockage that causes the person to have compulsive behavior even when it is against their will.   Remove the blockage and the person's compulsions are removed because their energy is in proper balance. The person may need to take further steps like being aware of bad habits and taking necessary action.   Don't confuse bad habits with addictions.

Q: I'm so inspired by learning about Chi Kung that I want to become a teacher so I can help others. How can I become a teacher?

A: Teachers are chosen, they don't choose themselves. For your best benefit, focus on being a good student and enjoying the benefits.

Generations of Shaolin Masters have passed down to us important time tested wisdom in the form of guidelines and rules for our benefit. These guidelines help us and others avoid unwanted results. Chi Kung is a powerful Art of profound depth. It is very irresponsible to teach it before learning to practice successfully, being instructed in how to best teach it and also to be able to help students that may obtain unwanted results when necessary. Becoming competent in practice takes time and cannot be rushed. Please have some respect for the Art, the wisdom of the Masters and consideration for your would be students. Realize that one cannot fully appreciate its depth after simply reading a book, watching a video or taking a class. Good teachers of Chi Kung are good students first. Good students typically aren't interested in being teachers but simply in practicing in order to obtain benefits in their own lives. Be sure to adhere to the 10 Shaolin Laws found in the Appendix and note several of them including, "Respect the Master", "Be wise", "Train the Arts diligently", etc. In order to get good results from practice simply focus on being a good student and enjoying your practice. As in all guidelines provided for your benefit please don't be reckless and disrespectful and think that you know better than the Master.

Good students, those who listen to their teachers and practice faithfully, are able to be taught further and learn more and more of the seemingly endless treasure that is the Shaolin Arts. Those who are not good students, including those who think they know better than the Master, deny themselves the opportunity to learn more. They are not taught further mainly for their own good.

Q: What Chi Kung techniques do you practice?

A: I practice the Chi Kung techniques that I teach.

Q: I've tried practicing Chi Kung before but I didn't get any results. Why would this be?

A: One must consider three factors necessary for successful results in Chi Kung practice. The Master, the Method (Art) and the Student. If any of these three factors are lacking it isn't reasonable to expect good results.

Q: How can I ask you more questions?

A: In my classes and seminars you can ask any question. Also, I can be reached through www.wondersofchikung.com . As I'm able, I respond to as many requests as I can.

Appendix I- TEN SHAOLIN LAWS

I've included the Ten Shaolin Laws in this volume because they are very important and shouldn't be ignored by practitioners of our very special art. The Laws were compiled and combined by my teacher from wisdom passed down to him from previous masters and texts on Shaolin Arts to make it a short and easy reference of important principles. These principles have proven to be important to adhere to in order to get not only the best results from practice but to help students avoid problems as well.

The Ten Shaolin Laws are non-religious, and transcend all cultures and races, i.e. people of any culture and race would agree that they promote values that are worthy and desirable. Laws, in the Shaolin tradition, are not meant to be punitive or restrictive, but as practical means to help followers achieve set aims and objectives; in this case to help them attain the best possible results in practicing Shaolin Chi Kung for health, joyful living, mind expansion and spiritual fulfillment.

There is no legal binding on the Ten Shaolin Laws; one cannot be prosecuted in a court of law if he breaks these laws. The binding is moral and they are not forced upon the follower; the follower accepts them because he chooses to because he believes they are helpful to him in his physical, emotional, mental and spiritual cultivation. If he breaks the laws, despite sufficient warnings, he may be asked to leave the Shaolin training, not as a punishment, but because the training is not suitable for him.

1. Required to respect the Master, honor the Moral Way and love fellow disciples as brothers and sisters.
2. Required to train the Shaolin arts diligently and to be physically and mentally healthy. (For those that are not yet healthy this gives them at least one goal in their practice)
3. Required to be filial to parents, be respectful to the elderly, and protective of the young.
4. Required to uphold righteousness, and to be both wise and courageous.
5. Forbidden to be ungrateful and unscrupulous, ignoring the Laws of man and heaven.
6. Forbidden to rape, molest, do evil, steal, rob, abduct or cheat.
7. Forbidden to associate with wicked people; forbidden to do any sorts of wickedness.
8. Forbidden to abuse power, be it official or physical; forbidden to oppress the good and bully the kind.
9. Obliged to be humane, compassionate and spread love, and to realize everlasting peace and happiness for all people.
10. Obliged to be chivalrous and generous, to nurture talents and pass on the Shaolin arts to deserving disciples. (Passing on the Shaolin Arts is only done by properly trained and certified individuals. It is irresponsible to attempt to pass on the Arts otherwise)

Appendix II

Comments from Practitioners

Shaolin Chi Kung has been treasured and practiced for over one thousand years because it gets real, beneficial results. The results of practicing Shaolin Arts are legendary in the history and literature of China. I've included recent comments from some of my students to give the reader some perspective on the breadth and depth of the many benefits that are relevant to people today and how obtainable they are with proper instruction. If you are interested I would encourage you to do internet searches on the results of scientific, medical and peer reviewed studies of the results of Chi Kung (Qigong) practice. There are many available and I'm made aware of more and more each week as some people alert me to them. Doing one's own research may provide greater encouragement for those who need it. Please note that most of my students don't come to me because of scientific research but from personal referral from my other students whom they know.

- Over the last couple of years I had noticed that my **fingers on both hands were becoming stiff** and did not easily bend. They also were frequently tingling. After practicing Chi Kung after learning from you only months ago, it only took a few days before I no longer had any difficulty bending my fingers. The stiffness and tingling were totally gone! Jennifer, Sitka, AK 2009

- I just can't tell you how happy I am to have learned Chi Kung from you. I've suffered from **Rheumatoid Arthritis and Glaucoma**. Since practicing as I've learned from you one year ago, I no longer suffer symptoms of Rheumatoid Arthritis. However, I noticed that if I don't practice for even 2 days that the pain and swelling will return. The solution is simple, do my daily practice and prevent the symptoms from returning. Also, my doctor has informed me that the pressure in my eyes has returned to optimum. I knew they were better before he confirmed that. I notice that my eyes look brighter and healthier. I'm so grateful. Alice, Sitka, AK 2009

- I took this course due to the strong recommendation of a friend. Since starting the course I am **sleeping better** and I have noticed more focus at work. I have recommended this course to others and I'll continue to do! Louise, Bellflower, CA 2009

- I took your course at the recommendation of 2 of my friends. Since starting to practice 3 months ago I feel that I am not as anxious about the little things that happen on a daily basis. In teaching there are so many times during the day that you run into stressful situations with small children, yet I feel that I don't get so frustrated and have more patience with them. I am reacting to things with much more calmness so **work performance has**

improved. I have much more energy during the day, and feel more positive. I have recommended this course to others and I wish everyone could take it.

You were an excellent instructor and I appreciated your kindness. You truly show the results of Chi Kung!! I am anxious to see myself six months from now! Susan, Lakewood, CA 2009

- Every time that I practice, whether in class or at home, afterwards I'm **calm and relaxed**. Thank you! Ellen, Signal Hill, CA 2009

- I have to stand for my job all day and I've had **pain in my knees** for years. One year ago I told you about this and you taught me a special Chi Kung pattern for this condition. The pain was gone in a week and one year later still no pain. Thank you! Anne, Long Beach, CA 2009

- I have to admit I was a little skeptical about what results I would get from practicing Chi Kung but I took your class because my business associates really encouraged me to try. Now I want to tell everyone what remarkable results I'm getting. Two weeks ago during our weekly class you taught me the Chi Kung Pattern "Pushing Mountains" and mentioned the many benefits from practicing it. One of them is how it is great for overcoming back problems. I have had **severe back pain** for years. In the morning I haven't even been able to bend over the sink to brush my teeth. After the first day of practice I felt improvement. In the two weeks since I've practiced this my back pain is gone! Wow!

The course was perfect! The benefits have gone beyond relieving my back pain. It has also contributed to balancing my **emotional response to high stress situations**. All this in such a short time! I'm definitely recommending this course to others!
Ericka, Long Beach, CA 2008

- I took your course in March and 6 months later I'm amazed at the results. I had a problem with **Migraines** for a long time. I've tried the various medications for migraines but haven't had real success with them. I practiced as you taught me and for 2 months I didn't get a Migraine!! For some reason I slacked off in my practice and they started to come back. The correlation between practicing your special Chi Kung and eliminating Migraine headaches is unquestionable. I'm back practicing again and I'm not going to let them come back. My husband and I are looking forward to your next seminar. Julie, Sitka, AK 2008

- I'm so excited I just had to tell you this. I took your seminars in March and May of this year and I've been practicing ever since. Over the summer my doctor told me I had a very large **Kidney Stone**. I was worried on how this might pass so I decided to practice the "Nourishing Kidneys" Chi Kung pattern that you taught me. After several weeks of practice I returned to my doctor to have him examine the stone. He couldn't believe it when he told me it was gone! I did notice when it passed but it wasn't overly painful. Another amazing story you can share with others. Thank you Sifu! I'm looking forward to your upcoming seminar in November. Alice, Sitka, AK 2008

- I took a Chi Kung course with Sifu Anthony in 2006 and I've been practicing regularly since then and I'm delighted with the results. I was amazed at the simplicity yet effectiveness of Sifu's instruction and I've experienced the results that I had hoped for. I have had abundant energy and mental clarity since taking the course.

As a Business Professor who studies Organizational Effectiveness, I'm always curious about methods that might enhance personal and professional development. I was very pleased to learn and understand how using Shaolin Wahnam's unique approach to practicing Chi Kung could do this. Furthermore, the principles explained and demonstrated in the course are directly relevant to the needs of organizations and the individuals who compose them. Human Resources and Management Professionals should strongly consider the Wahnam West approach to improving their organizational effectiveness.

As a bonus from the course, I learned the Shaolin approach to Zen. It is all about being simple, direct and effective. What Professional or Organization couldn't use more simplicity, directness and effectiveness in their actions and communications? Very few I suppose.

I highly recommend the unique but effective approach that Sifu offers, because not only do I understand it intellectually, I have experienced and embodied it.

Ronald Purser Ph.D
Professor of Management
College of Business
San Francisco State University

- I took your course for **Stress Management**, to reduce pain from my **Fibromyalgia** and for a **TMJ disorde**r. I have already felt positive benefits. Since starting I've been able to significantly reduce my intake of anti-inflammatory drugs and I'm noticing an increase in energy throughout the day. Tracy, Long Beach, CA. 2008

- For the last couple of years my doctors have recommended surgical removal of most of my insides in order to get rid of the **severe, chronic menstrual pain** that I've had. Within 2 weeks of learning from you my pain went away and it is still gone another month later. Wow! I can't keep the smile off my face from this. I look forward to another course with you and I'm absolutely encouraging others to learn from you! The benefits are emotional as well as physical. Marie, Long Beach, CA 2008

- I took your course to improve my quality of life, to relieve stress and to learn to have peaceful moments. As an executive in one of California's largest organizations I really needed it. I'm already recommending it to as many people as I can. During the short time that I have been practicing as you taught me I have noticed significant results that have improved my quality of life. These include—

  - I sleep soundly throughout the night without waking up.

  - My energy level is much higher.

  - I'm more focused at work.

  - I have a greater commitment to maintaining a healthy diet.

  - My **sex drive** has increased.

  - Others have commented that I look "less stressed".

  - The list goes on!

  Thank you for your expertise and leadership. I love the light and spirit that you share with others. I have benefitted from your talents tremendously and I appreciate you more than you realize. With gratitude, Ruth, Long Beach, CA 2008

- I've **lost 10 pounds** since starting this course only 6 weeks ago. I know it is because my energy is getting balanced. I enjoyed this course and feel the pacing was appropriate. I certainly am recommending it to others. Barry, Long Beach, CA 2008

- I took your course for a new experience and because I need major, new energy during this job changing time of life. You are a very patient, calming and knowledgeable teacher. I've already been forwarding information on your courses to a lot of people. Louise, Long Beach, CA 2008

- My mom convinced me to take this course to help reduce my **stress/anxiety**. I'm already recommending this course to others and I will continue to do so. Josh, Corona, CA. 2008

- I took your course for better health and energy. I'm already recommending this course to others. People have been saying, "Carol is getting in touch with her Chi". I'm looking forward to your next course. Carol, Long Beach, CA 2008

- As a Professional Chinese Acupuncturist I took this course both for my own health and for Professional Expansion. I will be directing patients of mine to your future seminars. Come back soon! Mary, Glenwood Springs, CO 2008

- I missed the start of your seminar in the morning because I had to go to the hospital emergency room. Due to your encouragement I attended the afternoon session and began feeling much better. By the end of the seminar

I felt the best that I have in a long time. Aspen, CO 2008

- I took your course to increase my energy level and overcome illness so that I could feel healthier and get off my medications. I will definitely recommend this course to several people I know that could benefit from it. I feel very grateful for all of the skills that I learned. J.R. Basalt, CO 2008

- I took this course at the recommendation of a friend to help me overcome several health problems including **shoulder pain and allergies**. My comment after the seminar? What a treat! K, Aspen, CO 2008

- Siheng Anthony. Thank you for coming to the brand new WIN Institute here in Basalt, CO to share the amazing art of Shaolin Chi Kung. You know how important this was to us. We look forward to having you here at our world class facility on a regular basis where we only provide the best to our clients. Chris. Basalt, CO. 2008

- As an attorney who's worked on a several pressure packed cases this year I needed this course. I'll be bringing my wife with me when you return for your next seminar. Bill. Snowmass Village, CO 2008

- I have been having **severe leg pain** for the last 4 months. This morning I didn't think I could even walk to get into your seminar today in

Henderson, Nevada. Thank you very much for making my day and getting rid of my leg pain. It was gone within an hour of practicing Chi Kung. I'm sorry I kept repeating all day that I couldn't believe my leg pain was gone but it simply seemed unbelievable. I am very grateful to get rid of it, more than you'll ever know. S. R. Columbus, Ohio 2008

- You made our day one we will always remember. We felt so comfortable and enlightened by your presentation and self confidence. The seminar exceeded our expectations. We hope we will see you again at another seminar or event. B.R. Columbus, Ohio 2008

- I had a problem with **insomnia** going back to 1999. I gave up on pills some years ago and wasn't sure if I would ever solve this problem. As a Surgical RN this had made doing my job a challenge. Within weeks of learning Shaolin Wahnam Chi Kung from Sifu I was sleeping better and getting the best rest I've had in years. My sleep now is deep and refreshing. I'm so grateful. -A. R. Long Beach, CA 2008

- I haven't been able to bend down on **knees without pain** for years. After only a couple of months of practice in your class I now bend on my knees without pain without even thinking about it. Amazing! -Pat H. Long Beach, CA

- For years I had serious problem with very difficult **monthly periods**. Since learning incredible Shaolin Wahnam Chi Kung from Sifu this has been reduced dramatically. Thank you! - Ashland, OR 2006

- Within 2 weeks of practice I was able to pass a lot of **Kidney Stones** with minimal discomfort. My doctor told me it was incredible. Thank you Sifu! L.A. Mexicali, Baja California 2008

- I've practiced and taught different types of Qigong for many years but now I know that nothing compares to Shaolin Wahnam Qigong. The deep levels of relaxation and energy flow I've experienced during and after a seminar with you are like nothing I've experienced before. Also, as a Medical Doctor I would recommend it to all my patients. Truly amazing! J.L., Ashland, OR 2006

- I took Sifu's class at the recommendation of my Doctor. I'm glad I did. When people ask me why they should learn this incredible and convenient art I tell them, "Because is works". It's amazing what results you can get from a simple 15 daily session. Pam H. Long Beach, CA 2008

- I took a Chi Kung course here in Las Vegas before but I can say that it doesn't compare at all to Wahnam Chi Kung. Las Vegas, NV 2006

- I took a seminar with you only 6 weeks ago and people already tell me that I **look 10 years younger**. Also, I feel great. M.B, Sitka, AK 2008

- Thank goodness for this course. I've already noticed the beginnings of positive changes. This class provided a great deal of information. Certainly I'll be talking about this and recommending it to my family and friends/co-workers. What more can I say without restating- Sifu Anthony certainly deserves the title, "Sifu". Chris S. Sitka, Alaska 2008

- If you come to Sitka again I hope to have my wife attend. I enjoyed your "positive energy" and methods of teaching. Thank you for the positive corrections to improve on the practice. Mike R, Sitka, Alaska 2008

- I attended this seminar because I have a **demanding job-extremely long hours**/often up all night and I've been finding it hard to maintain vitality and health under this level of stress. I feel that Shaolin Wahnam Chi Kung will help me achieve my health goals. Thank you for coming so far to teach us. The light in your eyes says more than any testimonial. Sharon S. Sitka, Alaska 2008

- I attended this seminar to be more healthy, happy, calm, and to enhance my spiritual life. (I have 6 children and suffer from migraines). I will recommend this seminar to others. Also, as a Christian I was very impressed with the 10 Shaolin Laws. I feel very at home with this and I know my spiritual life will be enhanced. Julianne S. Sitka Alaska, 2008

- I took this seminar to improve health, physical, mental wellness and to bring balance to life. Also, to **increase energy and physical stamina**. I'm already experiencing clearer thinking, I'm more calm and happier and feeling more alive. Thank you! What an honor to have you come here to share your art. Julie J. Sitka, Alaska, 2008

- I took this seminar to work on inner peace and improve general health. I feel my practice will relieve anxiety and improve energy. I enjoyed the simplicity of the art and I'm looking forward to the benefits. Matt S. , Sitka, Alaska, 2008

- I took this course to help me in Life Fulfillment and to maintain health and I feel that this will help me achieve this. Kent, Sitka, Alaska, 2008

- I took this course to improve my health on all levels and I would recommend it to others. I am a long time practitioner of **meditation** and this feels like a wonderful way to combine simple but powerful movements with a meditative breathing practice involving Chi. What could be better? A.H., Sitka, Alaska, 2008

- I attended this seminar for 2 reasons. To increase energy and clear my system of toxins that manifest in **sinus/nasal allergies**. The biggest reason I attended was to join/support my husband who is very excited, encouraged and hopeful about the practice. After taking this seminar I would recommend it to others. Mary K, Sitka, Alaska, 2008

- I took this course in a desire for health, happiness and more energy. After this course I feel my heart opened. I will recommend it to others! Tess H., Sitka, Alaska 2008

- I came to this course because a friend recommended it and now I will recommend it. I started to feel Chi and I was calm and relaxed after each session. Joann T., Sitka, Alaska March 2008

- I took this seminar for health improvement and I will now recommend it to friends, family and co-workers. Kevin K., Sitka, Alaska, March 2008

- I attended this seminar because I have seen my husband's health progress after taking another Shaolin Wahnam seminar down in Las Vegas. I'm always open to improving my life. Sifu, your energy is contagious. I enjoyed sharing the space with you. I feel energized and excited to experience continued Chi Flow. Looking forward to seeing you again at another seminar. Jenn L., Sitka, Alaska, 2008

- I had a serendipitous moment-a pleasant surprise- while standing in line at the Mellow Day Café, there was Zach who introduced me to this nice person giving a Chi Kung seminar over the weekend and I knew I had to come. And I'm glad I did! I'm excited to continue to practice. I'm grateful that Sifu Anthony was able to visit Sitka and share this gift. I know there are fellow Sitkans here who are interested in continuing the practice. Enjoy! Relax-smile from the heart. Just enjoy and let Chi flow. Kathleen M., Sitka, Alaska, 2008

- It was a terrific intro class and refreshes my practice. Zach L., Sitka, Alaska, 2008

- As an Olympic Trainer for over 20 years and based upon my experience practicing Shaolin Chi Kung learned from Sifu Anthony I can say that Athletes would gain a significant advantage over their competitors if they had the opportunity to learn and practice this special and rare Art. Bill, Sitka, AK 2009

- I've felt unhealthy since I had **strep throat** over a year ago and have a continual runny nose. I'm looking for anything to help me feel healthy again, like I was before the strep throat. I already feel the energy flowing and a release. I will absolutely recommend this to others. My family is already curious, interested and asking questions. I love feeling the energy flow. It makes me feel more alive already which is wonderful after struggling for over a year now with not feeling healthy. Thank you! Arika F., Sitka, Alaska, 2008

- I took this course because of concern for **arthritis** in my knees and somewhat in my hips. The knees are already much less painful even after standing for 15 minutes during the practice. I have learned more in the past 2 days than I have in 10 years! I already have 9 people in mind to recommend. Alice S., Sitka, Alaska, 2008

- I've studied with a Shaolin Master here in Las Vegas for years but I never knew or realized what "smiling from the heart" was and how wonderful it is or how simple and powerful Shaolin Chi Kung could be. Thank you! Richard, Las Vegas. NV 2007

- I returned to Oregon yesterday and did my first practice in my backyard this morning... It was about 7:30 a.m. and as I began "lifting the sky" the birds songs and I became one... as the practice continued, the birds came closer and closer... at one point, all of us blended... there was no me or them or the yard there was just the one... it was truly a beautiful experience... Thank you for sharing this with all of us... I hope to see you back in Sitka in Sept. And will keep you posted as the practice continues... Many blessings... Suzan, 2009

ISBN 978-0-578-02487-5

$14.95
ISBN 978-0-578-02487-5
51495>

9 780578 024875